An Awakening Soul

THE PRACTICAL NATURE OF SPIRITUAL GROWTH

by

E. Noah Sarath

Sunstar
PUBLISHING LTD.

An Awakening Soul
The Practical Nature of Spiritual Growth
by E. Noah Sarath
© United States Copyright 1998
Published by:
Sunstar Publishing, Ltd.
116 North Court Street
Fairfield, Iowa 52556

Cover Design: Irene Archer
Editing and Text Design: Elizabeth Pasco

LCCN: 97-061870
ISBN: 1-887472-44-4

Readers interested in obtaining further information on the subject
matter of this book are invited to correspond with
The Secretary, Sunstar Publishing, Ltd.
116 North Court Street, Fairfield, Iowa 52556
More Sunstar Books at: http://www.newagepage.com

To Nona Hamburg, who graced our presence long enough to bring me the teachings of her teacher, Maharishi Mahesh Yogi, and then too early left our world, but never really left.

Acknowledgements

This book could not have been written, nor the life it recounts be lived, without my wife Florence. She occupies yet the central place in this shared odyssey—beginning I know not when—now approaching its fiftieth year of this life.

The value of the encouragement and insight shown by the following people who read sections or all of the manuscript cannot be overlooked. Writing is always a lonely task and their contact and feedback made it possible to maintain focus and discipline. In this context, I thank Susan Hathaway, my first reader and supporter, Lucie Brown, Christine Edwards, Theodore Lundberg, Maria Ragucci, Patrice Sarath, Carmella Mosiello, Caroline A. Mellusi, Ann Spackman, Christine Booher, and Wayne Lavender. My thanks and apologies are extended to any I may have inadvertently missed.

Included with those mentioned above is the Fairfield, Connecticut *Bhagavad Gita* study group—that loyal band of readers who were particularly valuable over the years in helping me make sense of what often defied common sense. This small assembly includes on a regular basis, Ruth Ferguson, Mitchell Ferguson, Evelyn Rachinsky, Ingrid Carmel, Terry Nevas, Nancy Lundberg, Claire Rumsey, and many others who would come and go as their schedules permitted. There is no counting the ideas and revelations that went into this book which were generated at these meetings.

My gratitude to my son, Ed Sarath, cannot be exaggerated. His early encouragement evolved into editorial assistance, and then into substantial advice regarding content. Not only were his ideas helpful and necessary, but his approval increased my confidence in the eventual success of this effort.

Finally, I want to express a special thanks to editor Elizabeth Pasco. Her interest and concern for the quality of this material was equaled by her professionalism in ensuring it. This is a much better book because of her effort.

TABLE OF CONTENTS

INTRODUCTION

Writing this book has been like answering a call. The idea, once surfaced, kept gently forcing its way into my consciousness. In my own spiritual journey I found the lives of the great saints and mystics inspiring, and I often felt a transient exaltation identifying with them. But these individuals were widely recognized as extraordinary. What I wanted and needed but never found was the experiential story of an ordinary person, living a traditional family life but in spiritual darkness. One who, by the grace of God or the laws of karma, was touched by the awareness of a transcendental reality which brought him or her out of that darkness; and to know how that life was changed thereby. The knowledge that there are countless people who share that yearning helped me overcome my initial reluctance to reveal these aspects of my life to a general audience. At some point, I thought I would try to give to others what I so much wanted another to give to me.

In many ways, also, this book is about paradoxes and their resolutions. It tells of an unique spiritual awakening and journey which, despite its uniqueness, resonates and identifies with the spiritual awakening and journey of so many others, in ancient traditions as well as in modern life. It describes very powerful, subjective or interior events which, nevertheless, affect the outer person in subtle, even hidden ways. And, most importantly, it shows how the age-old paradox of humanity's aspiration for finding a meaningful spiritual life, and at the same time satisfying its secular needs, is finally resolved.

It is in this context that the idea of the practical nature of spiritual growth is raised, a contradiction in terms, or a paradox. Expectantly, one awaits an explanation upon hearing or reading of it, or perhaps a redefinition, to resolve it. But no redefinition is proposed; "practical" remains self-explanatory and "spiritual" is used throughout in its classical meaning: i.e. a completely subjective, nonsensory, transcendental aspect of human consciousness that permits recognition of higher values. These higher values include qualities of life not exclusively associated with the body, but a spirituality like that commonly identified with individuals living a cloistered existence, focused on God, and sheltered by the walls and rules of religious orders. More to the point, there are those who live in the religious life and those who live in the world, and modern life has erected a seemingly impenetrable wall between them.

This separation has been especially true in the Western world since the onset of the age of enlightenment in the 18th century. But even before then, when church and state demarcation was so blurred that religious and secular leadership often resided in the same person, there were monastic orders exclusively dedicated to realizing the spiritual life. Indeed, as early as the fourth century, Middle Eastern "Desert Fathers" would find even the "common life" of enormous monasteries restrictive of their spiritual needs. As Thomas Merton suggests in his precious little book, *The Wisdom of the Desert*, these individuals had to lose themselves, hermit-like, in a transcendent, mysterious Christian union outside the formal teaching of the Church that sheltered them:

> In many respects, therefore, these Desert Fathers had much in common with Indian Yogis and with Zen Buddhist monks of China and Japan. If we were to seek their like in twentieth-century America, we would have to look in strange out of the way places.[1]

As Merton indicates, traditional Eastern spirituality appears to Eastern modern eyes as unworldly as its Western counterpart. India, too, which gave birth to the world's oldest major spiritual scriptures, suffers this perspective as much as Tibet or China. So much is this attitude the case, it is not unusual for Western educated Indians to believe that India's backwardness is the result of the traditional Vedic ideas of nonattachment and withdrawal from the material world. Not surprisingly, this intellectual elite experiences the same spiritual conflicts found in the West.

This ascetic tradition, which finds expression in the Indian Sadhu, who, in wending his or her way to a Himalayan cave, (literally or figuratively) echoes the commandment Jesus gave to the rich young supplicant, "Go and sell everything you own and give the money to the poor, and you will have treasure in heaven; then come, follow me." In both cases, the understanding, although common, that spiritual life requires isolation, sacrifice and a special lifestyle is not correct. The subject of this book, then, is a new understanding: that the achievement and growth of spiritual realization and its practical manifestation is the birthright of ordinary people everywhere, no less than those drawn to the reclusive and ascetic life.

Inherent in all traditions is a place for these worldly mystics and saints, although this historic position has often been, as it is in the present, overshadowed and denied. Yet in the secular world, there are individuals whose lives, in ever increasing numbers, average or elevated from a materialistic point of view, are lived on a different spiritual level than other people; they are normal in every way, but exhibit certain qualities that mark their interior existence as different. Although the spiritual qualities of their reclusive cousins are often expressed and inspiring, these same qualities are hidden and unexpressed in their own consciousness.

Nevertheless, this spirituality, and the practicality of a life infused by it, has been noted both in the past and present.

No one has better described the psychological manifestations of this spirituality in modern man than the psychologist and philosopher Abraham Maslow. In his book, *The Farther Reaches of Human Nature*, he created a new designation for spiritualized people, speaking of them as "Self-actualizing individuals (more matured, more fully human)."[2] But if Maslow's concept is unique, its definition is consistent with traditional scripture. Maslow identified and observed exceptional people whom he studied to find just what it was that differentiated them in terms of self-consciousness, behavior, and their attitude toward the world. These are "people who are gratified in all their basic needs (of belongingness, affection, respect, and self-esteem)."[3]

Maslow found values inherent in their personalities, in their very being, or "B-Values," which are universally accepted as markers for the more exalted life: truthfulness, goodness, intrinsic beauty; transcendence, a sense of wholeness and integration; a sense of aliveness and spontaneity; an orderly, uncomplicated notion of justice; richness [not material] in a life which is lived without effort, with joy, self-sufficiency and independence.[4] It is clear to see that those who live a life characterized by these qualities are living up to their full potential, and they are more creative and happier. More than that, however, they can be said to represent a model of what a fully functioning human being can be.

Maslow's contribution, moreover, went far beyond describing the nature of the self-actualized person and showing the similarities of their lives with the saints or mystics of the past. He also finds and describes a religious or "peak experience" shared by all of them that provides a new understanding of the world and results in a personal transformation. It is this experience, the "core-religious" or "transcendent" experience that produces and sustains the "more mature and fully human" person; and it is this experience that underlies and sustains the world's religions. In *Religions, Values, and Peak Experiences,* he writes:

> The very beginning, the intrinsic core, the essence, the universal nucleus of every known high religion...has been the private, lonely, personal illumination, revelation, or ecstasy of some acutely sensitive prophet or seer.[5]

Although Maslow's concept of the peak-experience made the traditional spiritual, or mystical revelation a modern psychological paradigm, this experience is not new to Western literature. Indeed, when William James examines this occurrence in the latter part of the 19th century he is able to draw not only on the writings and reports from Christian, Buddhists, Hindu and Islamic sources, but also from contemporary and secular writers in the West.

In his classic study, *The Varieties of Religious Experience,* James's emphasis and orientation lay toward religious saints and secular mystics. Maslow, on the other hand, studied mostly lay people in all walks of life bringing to bear the observational and analytical techniques of the modern scientist. They came to remarkably similar conclusions, however, about how these experiences can be identified and how their subjects are transformed. One of the most important of these characteristics, for James, is its ineffability:

> The subject of it immediately says that it defies expression, that no adequate report of its contents can be given in words. It follows from this that its quality must be directly experienced; it cannot be imparted or transferred to others. In this peculiarity mystical states are more like states of feeling than like states of intellect. No one can make clear to another who has never had a certain feeling, in what the quality or worth of it consists.[6]

Maslow finds his subjects facing the same crisis of communication:

> Direct verbal description of peak-experiences in a sober, cool, analytic, "scientific" way succeeds *only with those who already know what you mean* [my italics] i.e., people who have vivid peaks and who can, therefore, feel or intuit what you are trying to point to even when your words are quite inadequate in themselves.[7]

James also describes a "noetic" [sic] quality, that is, knowledge or truth not acquired by the conscious or sensory intellect, another hallmark of the universal character of the mystical experience: "They are states of insight into depths of truth unplumbed by the discursive intellect. They are illuminations, revelations, full of significance and importance, all inarticulate though they remain; and as a rule they carry with them a curious sense of authority for after-time".[8]

Not surprisingly, Maslow finds this same quality in his studies. He writes of noesis in the context of a general survey relating peak-experiences to the reports of traditional religious episodes. But there is no mistaking the similarity of the events.

> In the cognition that comes in peak-experiences, characteristically the percept is exclusively and fully attended to. That is, there is tremendous concentration of a kind which does not normally occur. There is the truest and most total kind of visual perceiving or listening or feeling. Part of what this involves is a peculiar change which can best be described as non-evaluating, non-comparing, or non-judging cognition.[9]

Because this aspect of consciousness violates our modern understanding of the rational nature of the world, an understanding that limits us to a sensory perception of reality, we tend to shunt it aside into areas visited intermittently, if at all. And in those rare cases where the experience intrudes demandingly, we treat it as an aberration or go for therapy. It is clear, however, from these all too brief reports, taken deliberately from evaluations of secular sources, that there is a uniquely human characteristic of consciousness that connects mankind at a universal, nonspecific level; and when this connection is made, a new kind of physiological and psychological functioning commences in the individual. A style of functioning, it must be said, that is not only intrinsically valuable, but makes life itself worth living. This is the ultimate practicality of spiritual growth.

Writing about these issues from my long-term personal experience with them has its rewards but also presents great difficulties. Bringing these experiences to a conscious level enables one to acknowledge them again, and then when they are identified with like occurrences in others, the sense of their universality is enlivened. However, this effort also requires exposing very deep personal feelings and emotions involving an intense sense of the sacred that is all too easily trivialized. Spiritual transformation is the ultimate interior experience; to those unaware of its nature it is meaningless, and with those with whom it can be shared the inadequacy of language is unimportant.

A further challenge in presenting this material is reflected in a final but essential point. The expressions *self-actualizing or spiritual growth* designate the evolutionary processes moving toward enlightenment, a state generally accepted to be Brahman Consciousness in Vedic terms, or as union with God in other traditions. This is the goal of all spiritual practice.

The personal transformation as a result of the spiritual growth to be described in the following pages is far from complete. Although these pages include tastes and glimpses of this state of enlightenment, these tastes and glimpses are only personal milestones on a personal path. It is neither possible nor practical, very likely counterproductive, to try to evaluate one's spiritual progress on the basis of another's experience. Each one of us comes into this life as a unique soul with specific lessons to learn and problems to overcome. What has to be done to perfect and finish that work is different in each of us. Nonetheless, what we can all share and rejoice in sharing is our mutual experience in overcoming spiritual ignorance. That is our common first task; that is what, in the end, unites us all.

This book is divided into intermingled parts. They are not necessarily sequential in terms of time, but they describe different aspects of transformation growing out of their shared indivisible source. Chapter I describes the effects of peak-experiences in the life of an individual. It is an account of initiation, transformation and growth through the first six months of an extraordinary, hardly to be understood, odyssey that, before it settled into a new normalcy, seemed to offer a sense of a different and ideal mode of human functioning.

Chapters II, III and IV present a broad overview of a life lived in ignorance that is now seen through a new spiritual prism—one that reveals ancient patterns which over and over shape and repeat emotions, thoughts, and behavior until finally resolved by spiritual initiation and growth.

Chapter V shows how these experiences are associated with age-old spiritual traditions, traditions that established the mental and physical foundation for the experiences. This chapter also shows how the nature and history of this state of consciousness was revealed in the Western mind from generation to generation until its modern emergence.

Two nonsequential parts, Chapters VI and VIII, portray the coming of the teachers. Once embarked on a spiritual path, the seeker finds guidance and wisdom from all forms of teachers and from the most unexpected places. Unbidden, sometimes scarcely recognized, they light the darkest corners and steady the aspirant through the peaks and valleys of his or her often lonely interior journey.

Chapters VII and IX recount the blessings one receives through the daily contact with transcendental reality. They show how the fulfillment of family, social and economic life is achieved.

Chapter X deals with the sense of completion and reconciliation. Not completion in the sense of enlightenment as discussed earlier, nor completion in the sense one's life is over; but completion in the satisfying sense one feels when a person knows he or she has met life's responsibilities to family, self and society. Nothing is missing, there are no regrets, no wanting to do something over; rather, one sees one's life as the positive accomplishment of a purposeful effort. This is completion; this is the gift, this is the blessing of spiritual development. All possible disparate psychological, emotional and intellectual elements are integrated into one holistic worldview.

The Epilogue encapsulates the salient ideas of the entire book. Its chief concern is to show that the lessons learned through the experience of any one person on any one specific spiritual path have universal application for all seekers. It also indicates that although spiritual growth and transformation is the indispensable need for individual happiness, it is also the central requirement for social well-being.

Chapter One
Initiation

*I*t was the latter part of 1974 and I was just beginning to recover from a period of job failures and career setbacks. Layoffs, then lower level employment and not being able to use skills I long trained for, added to the stress of being the principal wage earner for a large family of seven children. These personal concerns were magnified by tumultuous national conditions: the destabilizing nature of the Vietnam War, the equally divisive nature of the civil rights movement, and the emergence of the women's movement which questioned long-held traditions regarding sex and gender relations.

In the previous several years, our eldest daughter, now finishing college, exposed her parents and siblings to the 1960s world of incense, marijuana and the Beatles—forcing us, like so many others, to come to grips with the parental nightmare of adolescent sex and drugs in a growing atmosphere that provided no responsibility or direction. It was into this mix that my son came home from college immersed in a program of Eastern meditation promising inner bliss, world peace and expanded consciousness: a program complete with a bearded Indian maharishi from the Himalayas who was to be the new world savior. I remember listening to a lecture at dinner one evening, not hearing a word, but thinking over and over again, "God! Now what?"

Considering this attitude, there was no logical or rational understanding of my progression to the practice of meditation.

After two largely uninspiring lectures by young, conservatively attired, unthreatening, meditation teachers, the matter rested, giving way to a surface, almost reflexive, response of resistance. Nevertheless, there was, as I now recall, a subtle tug, an ethereal beckoning in a way, to a further exploration of ideas I normally tended unthinkingly to dismiss. Then, after I finally agreed to be "initiated," a strange sense of anticipation developed and the idea of meditation, the nature of which was a complete mystery to me, became a source of excitement.

I never gave any thought to these inchoate impulses until many years later when I read Christopher Isherwood's account of his own identical episode. His report so clearly echoed what I felt, although experienced more than forty years earlier, that all those feelings flooded back into my consciousness. He wrote:

> Now that I had made up my mind to try it, the mere idea of meditating filled me with a strangely powerful excitement. I thought of it as an attempted confrontation with something hitherto unencountered but always present in myself. When I try to recall how I felt, I think of entering an unexplored passage in a house which is otherwise familiar to me.[1]

The reality of initiation did not equal the level of anticipation. My first meditation, as I now recall, was a pleasant event but also confusing. Since people are all so different in their response to this new level of consciousness, it is impossible to predict what reaction any individual will have. The overwhelmingly positive reports made in the lectures, the stories heard from friends, and the knowledge and belief one is doing something good for one's self fuels the expectation something extraordinary will take place. Although that did not happen, I had no feeling of disappointment. I remember a vague sense of accomplishment and satisfaction;

however, it was so vague in detail I would have been at a loss to describe my feelings then as I cannot describe them even now.

The confusion deepened over the next three days as I met with our initiator/teacher, Nona Hamburg, and other "meditators," as we now clannishly referred to and thought of ourselves. This meeting was to check our meditation and to clarify and share our experiences. Our teacher's main concern was correct meditation, which essentially meant understanding the role of thoughts during the meditative period and the nature of an effortless procedure with its proscriptions against "trying to meditate." Our concerns, on the other hand, involved an extreme range of experiences. One person reported feeling so energized after her evening meditation she spent hours cleaning her house, sleeping fitfully that night, then after her morning meditation going off to work feeling completely rested. But another had a diametrically opposite exper- ience; he complained that as soon as he began to meditate he fell asleep. Both experiences were normal, it was explained, because meditation "normalizes" the physiology and the body responds according to its needs at the moment. Over the years I found this extreme variation in experience not only common in different individuals, but also common at different times in the same person.

However, at the time I could hardly give credence to these reports. My own experience was one of a sense of nonexperience. I remember saying repetitively over the next several days, "but nothing is happening, nothing is happening." Then, on the final night of the checking course, I remember coming out of the group meditation aware I was holding a pencil in my hand. Suddenly, I realized I had had no sense of having anything in my hand during meditation, and then the thought came that I was unaware of my body during the final part or all of the meditation period. I found myself asking our teacher, "Nona, is that how I should feel, like I don't feel anything?" I do not remember her answer, and I know

now I could not have fully understood it then, but it was, indeed, a new state of awareness—a state transcending experience, simply being aware of awareness itself, a feeling but not a feeling of anything.

I left the meditation center that night with a strange mix of sensations. I realized a breakthrough of sorts occurred, that a different level of consciousness was reached; but as I tried to rationalize it and fit it into some intellectual paradigm (for that was the only way anything made sense to me,) the actual nature of the experience started to fade. I found myself thinking, "what was it that really happened?" I experienced the same exhilaration thinking of the event as I had felt when it happened, but that feeling was now tinged with confusion.

I first thought this was a singular occurrence, the result of meditation perhaps, but perhaps not. About three days later, however, a revelatory experience took place making it clear that something of great significance was happening about which there could be no misunderstanding. It was something I instinctively realized was the result of this practice and one that required understanding and guidance.

Carl. S. was our company president and when he entered the assembly and testing area of his small electronics enterprise the environment changed in an instant. An intense, driven man, his impatience and abrasiveness produced anxiety and fear in his employees. I was no exception to this and in my case this took the form of lesser or greater panic attacks. His habit was to hover over the employee while he or she was at work watching intently for a moment, often an eternity, before asking searching questions about why the person was doing this or that.

Our company made telemetry equipment for the National Aeronautics and Space Agency (NASA), and this work was done to very high standards and close tolerances. I was doubling as a test and repair technician at the time, responsible for seeing that the product met design specifications and repairing it if it did not. Testing was fairly straight forward because the specification parameters were set and the test equipment, although very sophisticated, could be depended on.

Repair was another matter, however. Troubleshooting electronics equipment is often as much art as science. This is especially true in equipment where shifting tiny coil wires or repositioning components can affect the results. Consequently, what fixes a problem in one unit will not always fix the same problem in another. There is a great deal of frustration in work when two units are seemingly identical, yet one functions properly and the other does not.

So when Carl demanded to know why repair units were piling up and passed units were slowing down, he would add to that sense of frustration and discomfort. This would trigger a response of anxiety and apprehension centered in the pit of my stomach that required a tremendous effort of will for me to maintain a modicum of dignity. I found myself stumbling in my answers to his questions, unsure of why I did one thing and not another, unable to explain why this sequence and not that was followed, and, finally, he would elbow me out of the way and start working on the units himself, reducing me to a condition of irrelevance.

It was little comfort that he treated everyone else the same way, although this lessened the distress of public humiliation. More significant for me, however, was my puerile reaction to this man. In my own mind, and in the evaluation of my colleagues and supervisors, I was not incompetent. And yet, my negative response to this kind of treatment was of lifelong duration and uncontrollable by will or intellect. I was aware of and distressed by this failing, but

I accepted it as part of my personality and more or less successfully compensated for it.

Therefore, when that day came, when for the first time in my life, I experienced a state free from that sense of anxiety and panic, it was nothing less than a revelation. A short interval, the actual time was impossible to determine, after a situation similar to the one described above commenced, I became aware of a strange feeling of deep calm. Although this feeling included a sense of being relaxed, it was not relaxation as normally understood. Rather there was a dynamic quality to it. It felt more as if I was floating in a quiet sea, but also as an integral part of that sea. The experience included an overwhelming sense of well-being. As I began to relate to Carl, I realized I was doing so from a level of equanimity that I perceived as unshakable. I told him what I was doing and why I was doing it with an authority I would not have thought I possessed. When he asked me why I did something, I answered that it was my judgment to do it that way, knowing he would accept that answer as, indeed, he did. This continued for a few minutes as I responded to his questions with a quiet but firm confidence. Complete control of the situation was in my hands. After a strange, but not strained, silence he looked at me quizzically, muttered a few affirmative words, and walked off.

Although the validity of this experience was unquestioned in my mind, it was underscored by the reaction of my fellow workers who were nearby and witnessed the interchange. None of them could have remotely shared the nature of my interior life at the moment, but they all were aware that something extraordinary took place, and they expressed that awareness openly. The full import of this event slowly made its way into my consciousness as the actual condition began to lessen in degree, or perhaps intensity. I experienced the reality of a level of life I could never have predicted or anticipated, one of great benefit, joy and transformation.

The encounter with Carl lasted less than twenty minutes and its full import did not surface immediately. As I went back to work I sensed that I touched, or was touched by, a hidden dimension of my being that represented a personal completeness of sorts; there was a part of me, now discovered, I never knew existed. But at the same time I felt a vague identity with a larger universe and it was this cosmic identification that put the mundane world in perspective. Anxiety, worry, fear and pain, all part of the world of things, are reduced to their deservedly minor statuses as one's consciousness expands to encompass the universe itself. But I was far from any concrete or intellectual understanding of any of this. I had feelings, sensations, vague impulses that provided insight, but these were shadowy glimmers of equally shadowy objects.

I finished the rest of that day with a divided awareness. I continued to do my work, satisfied I was relating and responding normally to my responsibilities. But, I was also acutely aware of a feeling of freedom or lack of attachment to my work, to social interaction, or even to what I was saying. In time, a diminution of the sense of expansion took place, accompanied also by a now familiar feeling of confusion and, perhaps, uneasiness.

Tugging at the back of my mind was the idea that "normal" people are not so "powerful," "detached," "confident," or whatever it was I felt. I really did not know and these were not expressions I would have used at the time. I felt an overpowering need to speak to someone about what was happening. Even so, after calling Nona later that afternoon, I realized I did not have the language to describe how I felt. To my great surprise and gratitude, however, I found that she did, and although we could not discuss this event in any depth then, simply being in contact with her and sensing her response tended to restore a semblance of balance.

In the next few months hardly a day went by without another example of this new mode of functioning. I knew intuitively that my meditative practice was the basis for what I could later describe as peak or spiritual experiences, and I hungered for explanations and knowledge. I found myself haunting the meditation center to speak with initiators and other meditators, both out of a need to maintain physical contact and to pick up bits and pieces of knowledge.

Even though the regularly scheduled Sunday night lectures were helpful, they seemed to fall far short of my needs. I was getting responses to my questions but not answers. This was not out of any devious intent, I am sure, but out of the requirement that meditation and its results be discussed in scientific terms: the effect of meditation on the nervous system, how the psychology is moved from negative to positive models, the lowering of blood pressure and respiratory rates and how all these beneficial results are related to the release of stress in meditation. This was all interesting and important, I thought, but none of it was speaking to the events in my life.

The Sunday night lectures, however, did provide an unanticipated benefit. It was there I encountered meditators who had knowledge of spiritual practices and teachings from other traditions, and they would ask questions about reincarnation, karma, enlightenment, cosmic consciousness, spiritual masters and the like. I had heard of these notions, of course, but only in the most superficial fashion, and they had no significance for me. Only a short time before I would have summarily dismissed these ideas as sheer nonsense. Now I listened and felt an eerie resonance with them.

We would not pursue these questions at the lecture, however, because, as I pointed out, the lectures were dedicated to explaining the teaching and the practice from a modern scientific point of view and, although I found that useful, it was strangely unsatisfying. The expression "strangely unsatisfying" is a good one in this context for the paradox it indicates. If I had heard lectures on meditation in the esoteric and mystical terms I was only now learning, I would likely have walked out of those meetings without giving them a second thought. Now, only several weeks into this program, it was the scientific explanation that left me impatient and discontented.

Because of this, a number of us would stay after meetings and talk, sometimes for hours, about spiritual matters. It was not that TM teachers and centers were unhelpful or disinterested. Actually, the opposite was the case, as I will indicate shortly. Later, at residence courses (weekend meditation retreats), I came into contact with other groups of more experienced meditators. Through these contacts I was introduced to a vast knowledge and literature that supported a multitude of spiritual paths and helped illuminate and explain the next years of my life.

Spiritual experience is one thing; understanding its nature is another. Maharishi Mahesh Yogi, the Indian monk who founded the TM movement, recognized early that the traditional language describing this experience was often incomprehensible to Western ears. To bring this profound Vedic wisdom to the West, he concluded, required recasting it in language Westerners would understand and respect. He did this by systematizing Vedic Studies in a program called, appropriately, "The Science of Creative Intelligence" and focused on developing modern scientific analogues for the ancient teachings. In this way he accomplished two main goals: making it possible to teach TM in all countries in a consistently uniform manner; and equally important, the removal (liberation?) of Vedic philosophy from its entanglement in hoary mysticism and the modern occult. I did not dispute the validity of the knowledge. My problem was the knowledge, as presented by the teachers in the center, did not address the esoteric nature of my experience.

This dichotomy between the nature of what I now began to think of as my spiritual path and the theoretical explanation of it through "official teaching" created a disjointedness in my relationship to the TM knowledge that was not resolved for several years. There was no doubt in my mind that this meditation program was correct for me. Maharishi's instruction through his teachers put me in the direct line of spiritual Masters represented by his teacher, Swami Brahmananda Saraswati. Although I did not understand it then, I was participating in a venerable tradition originating in Vedic times, thousands of years ago. I did not know what it meant to be a yogi; I did not know what spiritual practice meant or what enlightenment signified; but I knew I had found something sacred. At this point there was no thinking, just pure intuition.

Several months followed, when every day new examples would emerge, sharp and clear, of a more life-supporting activity. In meditation, spiritual or peak experiences became commonplace. At first, some of these experiences were frightening. The one that remains vivid in my memory was the sensation of separation. I had the powerful sense that "I" was apart from me. There seemed to be another entity that wanted to escape, that was trying to leave, and my fear was being unable to reunite. It was a real fear for I opened my eyes in panic and stopped meditating. Later I found this was a common experience of "witnessing;" something good was happening, I was told, a growth of consciousness and nothing to be feared. In the ensuing first weeks this experience repeated itself, although it diminished in frequency. With familiarity the intensity of the experience also lessened, and it became a normal part of my meditative life. I began to think of it as awareness of the soul.

Besides witnessing, another experience that started early and remains a constant feature of my practice was the realization of a suspension of breathing. In this case, I began to notice my breathing would stop for periods of time, just that, I was not breathing. I could not say for how long, but typically, I would become aware I was not breathing, however I was not holding my breath. I do not know how else to say it, I was not breathing but I was not holding my breath. Then, shortly after the realization of nonbreathing arose, I would take what seemed a compensating breath. But it was not a gasp for breath that would normally occur if one was being deprived of air; it was simply a resumption of breathing generally with the thought "I am coming out." In time, I associated this experience with an accompanying overall feeling of internal quietness. In my mind there was a clear recognition of moving to a different level of consciousness.

These and other glimpses of the transcendent in meditation were inspiring and valuable. Inspiring because even in those very early days I felt a very deep need was being satisfied, one I could not articulate and would have been embarrassed to try if I could as I did not have the spiritual language at that time. Though the scientific explanations did not appease this hunger—in this sense they were meaningless to me—they were valuable because they developed a confidence in the practice and a certainty of its goal. Since the purpose of any spiritual practice is the realization of the Absolute, or however one refers to this quality in life, achievement of this goal provides nothing of any material substance greater at the end of the journey than at its beginning. Progress is measured by a unique yardstick, one that measures hidden transformations in being, known only to the traveler—moving him or her to live a life supporting personal and social well-being, free of anger, anxiety, fear, envy and the other concomitants of an exclusive sensory-based existence.

The most striking and clearest encounters with this new interior dimension came in activity, both at work and at home. Its chief feature was the continuation of an anxiety-free state that translated into a state of equanimity. For as long as I can remember, my activity was dominated by a more or less anxious concern for its outcome, but now I began to approach my work with a new level of confidence. Faced with new assignments, I usually reacted with an uncomfortable, apprehensive sensation in the pit of my stomach. I noticed this feeling was largely missing; and when it was present it was in greatly diminished form. But even then it was accompanied by the vague awareness of another level of existence. I knew anxiety was not a natural or necessary response to a challenging situation, but I had no control over it. That the negativity of anxiety was being balanced spontaneously was not this well understood at the time.

This affected my work in a positive way. Since I was less fearful of failing, I was less reluctant to work in areas where I had little experience. I volunteered more easily for new assignments and more and more took the initiative in solving problems. This meant making decisions on my own with fewer consultations, thereby increasing the efficiency of the whole department. However, these external improvements were only minimally recognized because, in reality, my work always had included an acceptable level of competence. I did not change from an average employee to an exceptional one overnight. It was my interior life that reaped the greatest benefit. I was working with less effort and strain, with a greater sense of security and confidence, but beyond all that, the subjective and objective changes I was experiencing brought a new joy to my work.

Almost immediately, I experienced functional changes which were both practical and inspirational. My work, in part, required making comparative measurements in electronic telemetry equipment. Comparison between one measurement and another determined if the equipment was functioning correctly. The procedure was to make a measurement, write it down in its place on the test form, then make another measurement and write it down in its place and compare them. My habit was to stop and compare measurements after each step because I was not sure I remembered the previous step measurement correctly. At some point I began doing something differently, automatically, and without fore-thought. After measuring a step and writing it down, I realized I remembered the previous step number and could calculate the difference in my head. Just a simple thing like that, coming without expectation, made that job so much easier and much less boring. I was sure this new ability was another indication of "less stress in the nervous system."

I also sensed a greater ability to focus. It seemed I was able to concentrate more deeply on what I was doing and for a longer period of time. I noticed this for two reasons: first, because I was a person often working with a divided mind, that is, while I was thinking of my work I would also be thinking of external matters, personal problems or other areas of interest; and, second, the ability to focus was a parameter of psychological functioning medi-tation was suppose to improve, and I knew that. When I started to lose an awareness of time, being completely caught up in what I was doing without the usual distractions of extraneous thoughts, I attributed it to my practice.

Another quality I believed improved can be called an intu-ition of problem solving. Intuition in this context is defined in its conventional sense, the realization or knowing of something from no rational or sensory source. All problem solving depends on some level of intuition, but at what point that level is reached is so subjective it is impossible to quantify. I read reports of meditators who claimed an improvement in levels of intuition, and these reports triggered this recognition in me. This area of reporting is difficult to substantiate and so readily subject to suggestion, I doubt I would have thought of it had I not read those reports.

The question of psychological suggestion was not far from my mind since many of my experiences were similar enough, if not identical to, the benefits of meditation as reported in the popular press and the publications of the TM movement. Doubts would emerge, especially when the peak experience subsided and once again the familiar anxieties returned. I felt a deep sense of loss at those times. That this is a common experience of spiritual growth came to my attention much later when I heard a tape in which Maharishi addressed this very subject, apparently for meditators raising the same questions. "Do not doubt the experience," I recall him saying, "doubt the doubt."

What made it easy and natural to doubt the doubts were those objective changes in functioning that in no way could have been suggested. Even if minutely described, the essence of the experience could not be conveyed without the experience itself. For example, there are certain grating noises that cause distress to individuals. Almost everyone is familiar with the sensation and discomfort of some kinds of screeching like the dragging of fingernails across a chalkboard. A noise similar to that afflicted me at work; there was a workbench nearby that when moved emitted a sound which startled and bothered me terribly, especially when I was deeply engrossed.

One day I responded in a completely unpredictable way to that noise; I realized I was hearing it and I recognized it undoubtedly for what it was, but it was as if it were apart from me. I observed its beginning, its peak and its decay into silence, its entire cycle, and yet realized I continued to pay attention without interruption to a testing procedure I was conducting. As far as my response was concerned, there was no noise. To this day I do not react to those kinds of noises. Although I still am affected by and dislike loud and unexpected noise, I feel little discomfort or squeamishness.

At this time I lived through a kaleidoscopic period of personal events, resulting I was sure, from meditation. I remember sitting with a group of coworkers when a cup was jostled off a file cabinet; I surprised everyone, including myself, when I caught it about two

feet from the floor where it would surely have smashed. The incident immediately brought to mind the "fact" as I was told at a
lecture or read somewhere, that one of the benefits of meditation
was improved reaction time.

In those days also, I could be sitting quietly at my work area
when suddenly a feeling of well-being would surface; this was more
than the evenness of contentment or satisfaction which is sustain-
able and could be savored, it was more an uplifting, a positive
feeling of joy, a wave that seemingly came from nowhere and
returned to nowhere. The individual episodes would last only for a
second, if even that long, but they would leave a feeling of personal
expansion, that I was part of something infinitely larger than
myself. And somehow this produced a sense of security I never felt
before. The frequency of these occurrences diminished within
several weeks until they finally disappeared less than a year after
they began. But as I recall them now I realize the residue of the
experience, the sense of expansion with its gift of security had
spontaneously become a part of my life.

I felt then a curious intimacy with these emotions; I thought
speaking about them would violate a quality of the sacred I
perceived they represented, and it was some years before I would
mention them. When I finally did so, in the context of a residence
meditation course in an atmosphere of understanding and support
surrounded by fellow meditators, I found with great delight that
others shared this experience and almost everyone could identify
with it. Moreover, this sharing, which involved understanding and
knowledge, served to illuminate other events that occurred at the
same time allowing me to behold some very strange twists in spiritual evolution.

One of these twists concerned a long-standing nicotine addiction. I started smoking at age fourteen or fifteen, probably to satisfy
an adolescent need for acceptance. These early years are not noted

for clear thinking, but as one moves into adulthood their misdeeds and misperceptions normally drop away and are discarded. Cigarette smoking, however, is not a misperception nor a misdeed one simply stops performing; for me, it was an addiction I found almost impossible to break. When I began a lifestyle change focusing on healthy living and physical fitness, I found I could easily change my diet and enter an exercise program, yet I was completely frustrated by my inability to stop smoking. Finally, after many years of failed attempts, during which I often gave up trying, I stopped smoking for five years.

Although I actually quit smoking solidly, not one puff, for that period, I know now I never eliminated the addiction. Often during that period I yearned for a smoke. I recall many times consciously struggling against starting again and feeling relieved when the desire passed. The conventional thinking is that cigarette smoking helps relieve stress and calms the nervous system. But I went through some of the worst periods of my life during that time and managed to resist cigarettes as a crutch. Much later, to my dismay, and to the dismay of my family, I once again succumbed at a time when my life situation was relatively smooth.

I do not want to overstate the effect smoking had on my life. Because of lifestyle or genetics, I enjoyed excellent health and I rationalized there were more damaging personal activities. I was somewhat distressed that I could not stop such a personal destructive habit, yet in the back of my mind—no longer as an obsession—I knew I would stop smoking again. So, when I learned of the reports that meditators stopped or reduced the use of drugs, alcohol, and tobacco in larger percentages than their statistical population, I noted it as an interesting and positive factor, although one that would have had little or no influence on my decision to start meditating.

During the heady early days after initiation, when the feelings of expansion coinciding with my increased sense of security and confidence were most intense, my need to fight my cigarette habit vanished. I remember exactly how I felt; it simply did not matter. For the first time since young adulthood I was not concerned about pursuing a personally deleterious activity. I was being carried along on such a wave of positive feeling that negativity could not touch me. I had not lost my fear of smoking, yet in my expanded awareness I felt no apprehension of mortality—I did not think I was physically immortal, nor do I think I recognized an afterlife existence. Rather these became mundane concerns that lost their significance for me. Although these tidal waves of experience lost their intensity, the glimpse of what was possible remained a glimpse; however, more than a simple flash in the night sky that comes and leaves without a trace. This beam lit a light in the most shadowy corners of my consciousness never again to go out.

For all practical purposes, the negative feelings my smoking provoked became nonexistent, yet I continued to make periodic attempts to quit with the usual dismal results. One day in particular remains in my memory; the day I could not stop and actually gave up trying. I went to a weekend meditators' residence course with the idea of using that weekend as a springboard for a new nonsmoking attempt. I arrived at the course location, a beautiful rural setting in Connecticut, checked into my room, and was suddenly overcome with the desire to smoke a cigarette. The operative word is really "overcome." Despite everything I heard about how meditators reduce destructive habits, it seemed to me, at that time, in that room, more difficult to stop smoking than ever. I found myself rushing into town to buy cigarettes wondering about this tenacious demon, a demon I never fought again but, nevertheless, overcame.

About four years later, I began noticing something peculiar about my smoking pattern. First, I was simply smoking less; without thinking about it a pack of cigarettes would last more than a day compared with my usual pack to two packs a day. Then, I began to realize I would light a cigarette, take a puff and then let it burn away without smoking it. But when it occurred to me that I was no longer inhaling or inhaling much less, I knew something significant was happening. What it was came to fruition one spring morning in 1980, a full five years after I started the practice of Transcendental Meditation.

As we were sitting down for our morning coffee I noticed my cigarettes were missing. My wife had accidentally disposed of them in the washing machine with dirty shirts and such. For the first time in years I sat down for coffee without cigarettes and I did not care. But it was more than that. No effort was needed; there was nothing to overcome; there was no desire. In that sense, I did not stop smoking; *it was as if I had never smoked*.

This was more than a casual event in my life, it was an epiphany. I realized a window opened through which I could see and understand the world in an unequivocally different way; not only was the problem of an addiction resolved, but the personal struggle between a scientific and spiritual worldview was also resolved. The scientific explanations for my experiences of addiction were helpful but curiously unsatisfying. They spoke to my head with their talk of nicotine blood levels and addictive personality disorders. The Eastern and Western mystical explanations were much more satisfying, but I could only overcome my deeply ingrained materialist biases with much difficulty.

With this smoking experience, I saw at once the value and the limitations of the scientific analysis: it can explain the nature of addiction and develop coping mechanisms, but it cannot restore the organism to its pristine preaddictive state. I felt on the level of intuition, and I understood on the level of knowledge, that I was the conscious witness of the dissolution of a karmic bond. My most

serious spiritual doubts were buried with the ashes of my last cigarette, and the science/God dichotomy was finally put to rest. A
new perspective developed in which I realized the value of both
approaches to the understanding of life.

The classical scientific view of the world is eminently correct
and useful. But it is a world of the senses, the material world to
which it limits itself. In self-justification it claims existence only
for itself, denying validity to any other viewpoint. But in truth its
usefulness ends at its measurable limits. At nature's fundamental
level, where the tiniest particle dissolves into a field identified with
consciousness and uniting the universe, knowledge from the senses
must give way to new methods of understanding, one that can
comprehend the nonmaterial character of the world.

These thoughts and that experience were still well in the
future. I had now to deal with the effects of these changes on my
family. Our three older children were in different stages in their
college careers. Three teens and one pre-teen were still at home.
Our family, my wife Florence, my children, and I, were always inti-
mately involved in each other's lives so the momentous
happenings in my life could not remain isolated from them.

The dilemma was evident; my "transformation" was almost
totally subjective. They knew I meditated, but it was a practice
that simply involved being left alone. There was no physical or
verbal activity out of the normal range to indicate any change. If I
were more even-tempered, for example, it would not be so noticeable; even with three teenagers in the house I had periods of
evenness. I knew I could not speak to the children about these intimate psychological experiences, but to my disappointment, I found
I could not communicate with my wife either. She could not credit
the changes in my interior life, and the results of these changes in
my external life, to the simple practice of twenty minutes of meditation twice a day.

The seemingly obvious solution was for everybody to learn how to meditate, at least those at home with whom I was in daily contact. That this was a nonsolution to a nonproblem only became clear to me long after I proposed it. The children started easily, entranced by the assurances of their father that this simple technique practiced a few minutes a day would solve all their school and social problems. Florence's more reasoned resistance finally broke down after several months of nagging, and she agreed to give meditation a one-year trial.

In my simplistic understanding, I believed a few days of meditation experience would do for anyone what it had done for me. If not an identical experience, at least there would be glimpses and tastes of some of my new insights and behavior. I could not have been more wrong. The three teens at home started and meditated for different lengths of time before they stopped, and no amount of suggestion could convince them they saw "miracles."

Florence dutifully meditated for her year, stopped for a short time, then spontaneously started again and continued for almost the next twenty years before discontinuing the practice. Although her support for me in this "spiritual journey" seldom flagged, and she made a valiant effort to follow me to places she would never have gone alone, neither the knowledge nor the program seem to have any resonance or significance for her.

The realization that my oldest son, who introduced me to TM, was the only member of my family who could share this world with me was a disappointment. Though that disappointment was mitigated somewhat by the growing number of people I was meeting who understood and identified with what I felt, there was a sense of separation from those I deeply cared for.

The time came when that wave of euphoria carrying me along for the previous five or six months collapsed into a familiar anxiety.

This was my first encounter with what I thought of then as "my spiritual valley." In later years, however, I learned to refer to this experience by its most expressive designation "the dark night of the soul," after St. John of the Cross who showed its universal character to all spiritual seekers. The anxiety was painfully familiar, but it was no longer overwhelming nor accompanied by feelings of deep despair; it now shared my consciousness with the realization of an alternate level of being which never left me, although many times awareness of that level would hang by the flimsiest of threads.

Often for the next several years, my interior life alternated between contrasting modes of existence: on the one hand, there were diminishing episodes of anxiety, episodes lessening in interval, in length of time, and in intensity; and on the other, increasing episodes of equanimity interspersed with bursts of epiphanous feelings of well-being and joy. And also then the tenuous impression of being complete, being whole, of needing nothing more, arose in my awareness. It would be many years until that wispy sensation grew into a clear state of mind, but even in its infancy each hint of it was a source of comfort.

But nothing happened then, or in the many years of meditation to come, to eliminate the profound effect of those tentative contacts with transcendental reality. In later years, I thought of that period in more graphic terms: it was an ever-rising curve of peaks and valleys with the valleys of one period higher than the peaks that came earlier.

Chapter Two

The Wilderness Years

As I pass my 75th birthday, that sense of completeness I wrote about earlier assumes a more solid substance. In one form or another, all traditions recognize the changing stages in a person's life. The Vedic tradition perhaps defines most clearly these progressions because it has long recognized a goal, a purpose for life, to which these progressions lead. In this view, the student period prepares for the householder's life that in turn culminates in the final, spiritual stage, the intent of which is to move the soul forward in this lifetime, as little as one step or all the way to full enlightenment.

This final stage, referred in this tradition as "going to the forest" represents the period where an individual has completed all worldly responsibilities and can now allow attention to be directed solely toward spiritual needs. Although the idea of entering a forest may be more symbolic than literal in modern Western society, it is easy to see why an isolated retreat could have a positive spiritual influence. Achieving balance between worldly affairs and spiritual concerns, when surrounded by often raucous daily activity—especially as one's relationship to that activity steadily diminishes—is difficult. These mundane happenings can veil the natural tendency to enter this higher stage, even for those who are aware of it.

Yet, when this balance is achieved and the spiritual nature of the individual emerges and strengthens, it is the worldly affairs that start to take on an ethereal quality, and the spiritual life becomes more substantial. In this way, whether one goes to the forest or stays in the world, the forest and the trees are both clearly seen. As I contemplate these ideas, I am struck by their impact on my situation and begin to see the deeper meaning to my sense of completeness.

My role as husband and father retains its form, but has lost its content. I know I am loved by my family, and I am sure I will be missed if I passed from their lives today. But the direction those lives have taken will continue despite my absence; their material and spiritual unfolding have long depended on their own interior resources. Whatever contribution I was able to make I made, and their lives are now their own in all respects. I realize now if there is any further need for me in this world, it comes from the fullest possible expression of my spiritual identity.

My continued presence can only be a reminder of my sincere desire for their well-being. The success or failure of this desire is so much an amalgam of the infinite interplay of all our natures that only God knows what is cause and what is effect. Our love remains, and it should no longer be influenced by what we do for each other.

In the same way, all my former material interests have diminished. Certainly, the emotional aspect of these interests has lost its hold. But this awareness leaves me with more a sense of freedom than a feeling of despair that my life was losing the source of its savor. It is easy enough for a person in relatively humble material circumstances to blithely declare that no matter how exalted a person may be in terms of wealth, power or social acclaim, none of it matters, least of all to the person affected, without the awareness of one's spiritual being. I say this, however, with the confidence of long observation. But I say with even more confidence that with the experiential knowledge of one's spiritual being, neither wealth, nor power, nor social acclaim can throw a brighter light into one's existence.

The accomplishment of this spiritual expression gives life joy, gives it meaning, and provides daily fulfillment. This is what completion means to me; but it does not mean an ending. It is on this basis I contemplate new beginnings. I am acutely aware of the present with no attachment to the past nor sense of the future. I watch it unfold as I watch myself unfold. But in a strange way, the past also changes in the process. Not the events of the past, not the facts of life; however, what they meant, and why they occurred, take on deeper meaning and reveal patterns that enliven the personal experience of the order and intelligence of the world.

The unblemished sense of satisfaction and accomplishment I feel now, so often accompanied by a serenity I never tire of, serves also to disconnect me from what I can only call my previous life. It is stunning to me that my present situation could emerge from such a dark night. I can no longer feel, but I can truly remember, the anxiety, fear, hostility, envy, mean-spiritedness and dishonesty that plagued my life. I know my family and friends will shrilly accuse me of gross overstatement. But that is because these feelings and qualities were controlled and unexpressed for the most part.

I say on my own behalf, I recognized their destructive aspects and consciously tried to live a positive and socially beneficial life. I especially felt keenly responsible to be a model for my children, which was an added incentive to act properly. And also, in this context, the qualities I often struggled to emulate in terms of self-less and constructive behavior, were as much a part of my wife's nature as her breathing. I could not countenance losing her respect or affection.

I knew the difference between right and wrong—it is not really a difficult judgment to make—and I struggled to live as a socially constructive person. To my credit and satisfaction I was largely able to do that. But that struggle ended, for the most part, after my spiritual practice began. As anxiety levels decreased, those negative tendencies slipped away. Further, I became aware of another insight into that changing level of understanding: I now performed positive social activity easily, and without my former self-congratulatory attitude. The great wonder is not only that this transformation could take place, but that it could take place through the use of such an exquisitely simple spiritual technique.

Spiritual vision allows one to look at his or her life as one looks at a topographical map. Hills, valleys, dead ends and false starts, quietly flowing rivers and rushing violent rapids, are all exposed and clarified from this vantage point. I will later describe the importance of my marriage and the role my wife, Florence, played in enabling me to acquire skills and realize a potential the sharpest psychic scalpel could not reveal. On this map our marriage would emerge as the broad highway that ran straight and true from its first access to its fulfillment. But other details also surface: strange and contradictory events that have only their existence themselves to wonder at and their meaning food for esoteric speculation.

I remember my earliest days as chaotic, but also predictive of what I think of as a disastrous childhood and adolescence. On this map they would appear as a wilderness area; no signs or guideposts and only now a hardly discernible footpath ending in a somewhat more purposeful roadway. My first faint recollections are of the dominant role my mother played from these beginnings, with father, grandparents, aunts, uncles and siblings sporadically entering and leaving my life without significant impact. There was also, as I think of it now, an inchoate sense of self. I do not know how typical this is of preschool children.

Until late adolescence, my father was always a shadowy figure. His work required a lifestyle that provided minimum presence and influence. He was a bookmaker, a gambling promoter, and a compulsive gambler. This is akin to an alcoholic tending bar or a drug addict dealing drugs. The mix is ruinous, but New York City in the 1920s, his working environment, was so awash with bootleg money that the loss and gain cycle seemed endless. For me, he was an authority figure felt from afar. He slept most of the morning and went to "business" in the early afternoon. That window of opportunity to see him was not the most pleasant of times because of a habitual irritability. Nevertheless, I understood even then he was the one to please and I worked for his approval. I sensed this was also my mother's approach to him, and as I grew older this early understanding proved completely accurate.

Very early, my mother and I fell into a conspiratorial arrangement regarding my father, and this lasted all his life. He learned from us only what was absolutely necessary. Most household requirements she could handle, and he happily left to her all child-raising decisions, including my schooling. I quickly learned that my mother was the one to deal with for all my needs, and if there was something for which I did need my father's acquiescence, she would be the intermediary. One consequence of this was that because of mother's willingness to judge from her heart, I was able to wheedle many inappropriate decisions from her; it is not to my credit that I shamelessly manipulated that quality.

This pattern was established by the time I entered school, and it was constantly reinforced from those elementary days. The structured setting of school, however, rather than providing some coherence for my life, served as a backdrop to emphasize its inconsistency and unpredictability. In third grade I was put in what would now be called a special education environment. It consisted of one classroom and teacher with groups of differently graded students. Not only were we working in small groups in our various grade levels but we also had special nap times and snacks. We would pull out cots in the early afternoon for that special time, and we all knew how we differed from other classes.

I do not know if I was put there because of behavioral or learning problems. But I suspect the former; I had to bring notes home requesting my mother's presence so often that it seemed as natural to see her at school as at home. Moreover, I do not ever recall an inability to do my school work. Nor do I remember learning to read; it seems to me that I was always reading naturally and with little effort. I think of this ability now in the way I think of children with an extraordinary talent in music, or mathematics, where practice and perseverance can hone and fulfill, but by themselves can never create. I believe now, there can be no better understanding of this common phenomenon—these special abilities in children—than that they are examples of spiritual influences beyond our rational ability to penetrate.

I spent a year in that class, a time not without its share of misadventures. But for whatever reason, and unlike many of my other classmates, I went directly into a "normal" fourth grade. In a way, this grade was a milestone as it revealed certain motifs in my behavior that were to repeat themselves over and over for much of my life. I must have been very unhappy in school then, because even now I can recollect the fantasy world into which I would retreat.

I was determined to do better, and I remember being positive and enthusiastic about the opening of school. The significance of this attitude lay in my inability to maintain this enthusiasm for any length of time. Of course, I only recognize this significance now, as I sometimes speculate about its origins. Inevitably I would lose interest, perhaps from simple boredom, but often, too, a singular event would occur that would take the joy out of school work. I can appreciate the spiritual implications of this "personality" characteristic only now, as it perfectly illustrates the idea of the transitory nature of material satisfactions. And I believe the repeating patterns of the events of this life are lessons carried over from some mysterious past (possibly from one life to another) until they are finally learned and are suffered no longer.

Over and over through the years I found that my reward for creativity and initiative was ridicule and discouragement. It was in fourth grade that this event first surfaced. We had an elderly male arithmetic teacher who would come into our class only to teach this one subject. We were learning fractions and I understood them readily enough so there was time to play with the numbers. I found a way to solve them differently from the method he showed us, and I remember my excitement and pleasure as I got the same answer both ways. When I proudly showed him my discovery I was shocked at his response. He scolded me terribly and insisted I do only what he taught and accused me of showing off. Of course, I could not understand what I did wrong. Not incredibly, I have no recollection of doing any other arithmetic for the remainder of that school year, but the memory of that scolding remains.

It was also in that 4th grade classroom that I discovered more than a modicum of control over my world. I had a rich imaginative life fed by wide reading and Saturday afternoon movies. One day I decided to skip an afternoon class, a truly daring idea. The decision may have been impulsive but its implementation was well planned. Normally, we returned from lunch at home and mingled outside the school entrance until a teacher or custodian opened the locked doors and let everyone in. The person opening the doors remained inside until the last person entered, and after a cursory look outside would close the doors. These doors could not be opened from the outside and any latecomers would then have to go to the school's main entrance.

Near these doors was a barred recessed basement window and I knew when I squeezed into that recessed space I could not see the school doors. I reasoned that a person looking down the street from those doors could not see me. More than that, I believed by closing my eyes and remaining motionless I could not be seen. I really imagined I could be invisible. As the group of students moved into the building I hung back and slipped into my place. I can hear that door click shut even now, and I remember the feelings of exhilaration and freedom when I stepped out of my hiding place into the deserted street.

My plan worked perfectly except for a "minor" miscalculation. I never dreamed my mother would come to school on an errand. I cannot imagine what she thought when she went to class and discovered I was not there. The real seriousness of what I did was brought home to me when a policeman found me meandering in a nearby park and brought me home. I never found out if he was looking for me or if he simply realized I should have been in school. I knew it was a calamity when I got home and found my father there.

If I were punished I have no recollection of it. But I do remember a feeling of accomplishment. The object, in fact, was not to get away with anything but to break out of boundaries, although surely it was not that well thought out at the time. No matter how it ended, I am sure I could not have kept that adventure to myself. Indeed, my boldness and ingenuity and sense of self-control in this event provided a sharp contrast to a developing sense of general personal inadequacy.

It was around this time, I realize now, that these contradictory traits in my personality entered my consciousness. A continuous indecisive struggle ensued between an awareness of myself as an incompetent, unworthy, even undeserving person and a person of intrinsic value, intelligence and esteem. My life would seesaw back and forth as these conflicting psychic constructs would vie for ascendancy and find reflection in the events of my world.

Although I finished elementary school in due course, this was not a foregone conclusion, as in fifth grade my mother had to go to school and intervene so I would be promoted. As I prepared for junior high school, the pattern I spoke of earlier became fixed and clear. Most of my classmates, who were also neighborhood friends, were going into what was called "Rapid Advance" classes. I was going into a regular seventh grade class that was on a lower academic level. True to form, as I entered this new school I was determined to do my best work and once again I approached these responsibilities with enthusiasm. It was not long before that effort had its usual rewards, and I was transferred into the Rapid Advance classes, only to once again fritter away those promising opportunities.

The disciplinary problems I faced in elementary school were exacerbated in this new environment. My approaching adolescence, the more frenetic pace of junior high school, the difficulty in adjusting to new social conditions, threw me into a state of confusion and apprehension. This condition mirrored my home life. In 1934 the country was in a deep economic depression, and we were not untouched by it. My mother began a small home business selling ladies apparel, and my father tried to continue his regular "work." The heady days of the 1920s were long gone, and even in those days he was somewhat of a peripheral player; now, in these newly desperate and socially conservative times, making a living as he did lost all its social approval, not to mention its legality.

Despite these circumstances, my parents managed to maintain a household that sheltered, clothed and fed us all through those depression years. Only after I became a parent myself, struggling to provide for our family, could I realize what those days were like for them. Often, when faced with those fears, I thought of other parents I had seen in the early 1930s, huddled with their children and furnishings on the city streets after eviction. I cannot imagine the total trauma of that situation or the fear of its prospect. Even with the elaborate social safety net now in place because of those times, financial insecurity is a difficult and frightening experience for any family.

As an adolescent, those thoughts were far from my mind as I was centered on my own concerns. Because of my parents' preoccupations, I found myself virtually free from supervision as long as I did not call attention to myself. Interaction with my siblings at that time was so minimal I have no recollection of any relationships but of the most trivial nature. My older brother was, himself, then preparing to quit school but I did not know that until much later. I learned I could pass months at a time with little or no accounting for my activities. For a person of my nature and with my lack of self-discipline—I was only twelve, after all—this was a formula for disaster.

I went to school every day at first. I brought my books home but did my homework as the spirit moved me. I realized early on my mother accepted anything I said, and I had to answer only to indifferent teachers for my school work. I found it easy to skip school and soon mastered the system. My teachers and, presumably, the administration would accept any excuse to avoid contacting parents. From her side, my mother would accept any excuse to avoid getting involved with my school life. If my marks were not good, as they often were not, all I needed was to tell her I would do better next period and she would sign my report card. We both knew my father would not see it. He never asked.

As night follows day, my enthusiasm for school slid into disinterest, and as I did less I fell more and more behind in my work. Predictably, I was transferred back into regular track schooling after that first year. How I managed even that level I do not know, but I was promoted to regular eighth grade. Although this was a fateful step, I doubt if I could have understood its significance even if I were told. There was little counseling and with no parental contact, neither my mother nor I knew I was being shunted away from an academic high school to a vocational high school. If there had ever been any opportunity for me to have a productive early formal educational life, it was now lost.

We lived in a reasonably coherent lower middle-class Jewish community in the Upper West Side of Manhattan. We were part of that community, my mother more than my father. My mother had many lifelong friends, and my friends by and large were their children. Unlike my older and younger brothers, however, who were well integrated into their age groups and maintained that early bonding all their lives, my interests and activities began to diverge from my group as soon as my earliest teen years.

I was not lonely, nor was I a loner, but I was an anomaly. My mother liked to say that had I not been born at home she would have believed she was given the wrong infant. Depending on my prevailing state of mind, I accepted that statement as either a compliment or with chagrin. I now think of this time as an existential expression of the myriad of contradictory influences directing my life.

It is here that the role of karma and past life influences emerge as a compelling concept. This idea is so clear and charming because those impulses and desires and fears that generated that behavior surfaced in my earliest memories and remained with me all my life, never understood, but noted by my often futile efforts to overcome them. Modern science can try to explain their presence but only the flames of my spiritual practice can explain their demise.

My junior high school days held no surprises. Somehow I managed to move from one grade level to the next, although the end of each year was a crisis period. Incrementally and inexorably, I started to become separated from my community associations as our school situations diverged. The different academic tracks meant that my childhood friends were going on to a high school that was preparing them for college, or for work that required those kind of skills. Although I was formally offered the choice of high school when that time came, any thought I had of going to an academic school was discouraged. With my mother's reluctant agreement, we decided I would go to a vocational high school. No one else I knew from my community was going to that school.

Both my parents were children of Russian-Jewish immigrants, and my only living grandparent, my father's mother, was living with my aunt in an observant Jewish home. But my father was nonobservant with strong "anticlerical" feelings regarding organized Jewry. My mother adopted my father's position and in lieu of any reason to do otherwise, so did I. But despite these attitudes, I always accepted myself as a Jew and, indeed, accepted that fact as a positive quality, although I knew little then of the achievements and the cultural contributions of the Jewish people.

The significance of this was that my high school drew students from virtually every ethnic community in the city, except mine, and I remember an ill-defined sense of not belonging there. My self-imposed poor school experience was always generated in opposition to the attempts by the important adults in my life to improve it. And not only the adults; my peers were generally positive about their schooling, an attitude that I recognized and often envied, but that I could never really feel. But here, in an inner-city school, there was minimum social interest in the school and its students, and parental influence was likewise nonexistent. And, in fact, a large section of the student body was only marking time until they could legally drop out.

If I started my journey to disaster in junior high school, if not earlier, I completed it in high school. But now, for the first time, I became conscious I was adrift in dangerous waters. Not physical danger so much, although in this tough all-boys environment there was always that prospect. It was a different danger—all the methods of deception and dissembling that I successfully developed in junior high were to find full expression now.

A vague uneasiness arose that I was heading down a self-destructive slope with the sense that I could not stop or reverse that slide. Despite the entreaties, guidance and well-meaning injunctions of my family and general community, I was discarding values with which I was well acquainted. I heard expressed time and again the importance of education and responsibility to family and community. These notions insinuated themselves into my consciousness, and intuitively I felt their presence. But rather than understanding these contradictory stirrings as positive impulses, I thought of them as weaknesses to be rejected and overcome. With a mixed feeling of exhilaration and despair, I recognized it was my own maneuvering that had put me into this alien place with no chance of turning back. I am describing these feelings as I remember them with greater psychological clarity, I am sure, than I could have possibly known at the time. The cogency of the emotions they provoked, nonetheless, remain with me.

If a system were designed to provide fullest rein to the negative inclinations of undisciplined adolescence, it reached perfection at this vocational high school. Attendance was taken only in home room and once marked present there, the student was considered present for the school day. Although, once in the school building—located in Manhattan's midtown theater district—a student was not permitted to leave the building until the end of the school day, it was possible to skip class without the absence being noted on one's report card.

It was not long before I and several like-minded companions found a way to sneak out pretty much at will. At that point, however, early in my first high school year, I was not yet completely incorrigible and my immediate future was entirely in my own deficient hands. When I left home in the morning to go to school neither my parents, nor my siblings, nor my friends had the remotest idea of the world I was entering. Without any restraints, the downward slide became a free fall as I found the relatively firm social structure set up by home and community simply did not exist in this environment.

Gradually, I began to spend more and more time out of school as I discovered how easily I could avoid those adults who had a formal responsibility for my actions, i.e. parents, teachers, relatives and neighborhood friends. This gross disobedience was bold behavior for me, but my early trepidation was quieted by peer companionship and an ease of accomplishment. To the same extent my formal education was neglected, my street knowledge flourished. All of us became expert at stealing and lying. I received twenty-five cents a day from my mother for my personal needs; ten cents went for subway fare and ten cents for lunch with the "leftover" nickel for myself. I never had to use it for those purposes, however, as we stole lunch from open food carts and sodas from the slow moving beverage trucks that lumbered down crowded side streets.

At every traffic light, the rear of stopped trucks offered hand and foot holds for monkey-like teenagers to grab and ride many city blocks before being chased by an alerted driver. Free transportation on the subway system was equally available because of the many unmanned subway entrances. These used large gate-like revolving turnstiles and in those days I could easily shimmy under the bottom rail. Before long I was able to locate enough of these stations so I could always get home if I had no money.

As the first year of high school progressed, I grew bolder and more confident. It seemed, as I recall, that no matter what explanation I offered for my behavior it was accepted. I no longer needed the support of my friends to skip out, and often I found myself alone in the city. I began to steal more substantial items as I would open the doors of unlocked cars to rummage through their glove compartments. I remember once finding a camera and another time a pocketbook which yielded a few dollars. I was always on the lookout for something I could get away with, and I often found something. I never got caught. The end of my normal school day would be about three p.m. and if I returned home by four, and my mother was home, I checked in and went out to play. I was, after all, only fourteen years old.

I realize now I was then living two lives. It was natural for me to come home from that wild "school" day and associate with my traditional childhood community. But now this activity was tinged with a strong sense of discomfort. I started to discern a difference in the quality of my experience and that of my boyhood friends. They had a school life in common that I could not imagine. They spoke of academic subjects I knew little or nothing about, even if I recognized their names. They spoke of and evaluated their teachers with a familiarity I could not fathom; I do not think I could have named more than one or two of mine. They spoke as if they had goals and purposes and as being part of something that gave meaning to their lives. From somewhere deep inside me the realization arose, with a distinct feeling of despair, that there was something essential to my being that was slipping away from me and I could not stop it. It was about this time that I began my lifelong habit of trying to understand the world and my relationship to it.

I do not remember over what period of time these inchoate feelings made themselves felt, but I sensed clearly the destructive nature of my activity. Toward the end of my first high school year, I started to attend classes and managed grades high enough to get myself promoted. Not only did I miraculously salvage that school year, but also my father was able to get me a kitchen job at a summer camp; my younger brother's camp fee was waived in lieu of my pay. It appeared, once again, I escaped unscathed from my self-destructive behavior. No one had the slightest idea of the way I lived the previous six to eight months. I was permitted, by whatever power grants this, to make a fresh start. Not for the first time, nor surely for the last, was this permission granted. Only now can I properly give thanks.

This summer experience introduced me to a new social dimension as I worked in a structured setting with a more adult population. For the first time I was part of a group with a common goal and a specific responsibility that was valued. Maintaining a clean kitchen and dining room large enough to provide three meals to 250 or 300 campers meant few breaks during the day, and as the least skilled and most easily replaced person, I had some of the worst jobs. I did not always rise to the occasion, but for the first time in my life I found sympathy and support from fellow workers who treated me with an easy camaraderie. More than once, one of them would help me clean the huge cooking pots after his own work was done so I could finish the day at a reasonable hour. I remember yet the feeling of satisfaction I felt after the day was over, and I would sit with them listening to adult talk and thinking I was "someone," especially since many of the campers were my age and thought of as "kids."

The two months away from the environment and temptations of the city provided enough rest and distance for me to think a little more clearly about myself. I took to heart the supportive things my coworkers said to me as we parted, and I began to feel a sense of worth. I approached the coming school year with the same enthusiasm and personal resolve to do better that marked other times, perhaps now with a little more confidence because of my positive summer. I attended classes regularly at first and started to ask questions and show some interest.

On one occasion our teacher was having trouble explaining the nature and function of a metaphor. He assigned us the writing of one for homework. I felt clear about the idea and I carefully crafted what I thought was a beautiful illustration. When he asked who wanted to read first I immediately answered, and when he called on me I was primed for praise. He said it perfectly illustrated what he wanted, but he wanted us to write it ourselves, not to copy one from a book. When I tried to protest that it was my own creation he cut me off and called on someone else. I was humiliated, resentful and angry but, nevertheless, at the end of the period I went up to him to explain it was really my own thought. All he said was: "I don't believe you." I never went back to that class.

Things went downward from there. I hated school but I did not revert completely to the reckless behavior of the previous year. Now there were some positive, albeit weak, forces mediating my behavior, stemming from the growth of my constructive summer, and rather than mindlessly rebelling, I began to think of other options. In some way I learned I could transfer to another school and I thought if I could do that it would provide the fresh start that invariably energized me.

If the test of correct action is the ease of its accomplishment, then my transfer to Metropolitan Vocational High School should have proved my wisest move yet. No sooner did I indicate what I wanted to do, then the transfer took place; and so rapidly I was sure my "old" school was happy to get rid of me. I can not understand how this could have happened without my mother's approval, but I have no recollection of her involvement. I do remember trying to explain to her why this new school would be better for me, although it was a much farther distance from home, but I am not sure if this was before or after the fact.

This move, needless to say, did not bear out the adage of correct action. My school life was no better at Metropolitan than it was before, and perhaps worse as in this new school I was a complete stranger. I remember my confusion, alienation and despair as I tried to escape into an unsatisfactory fantasy world. I somehow finished the 1937 school year and spent an aimless summer at home.

In the fall, I attended one or two days of the start of the new school year, but I was so dispirited I could not force myself to continue. I would leave the house in the morning as if I was going to school and return at an appropriate time in the afternoon. I would spend my mornings riding downtown on the subway picking up discarded newspapers in the downtown stations and returning uptown to sell them. When the billiard parlors and bowling alleys opened in the late morning, I would help clean up, then later rack pool balls and set pins as players trickled in. My companions were now gamblers and small time "wise guys." I hung around the daytime poker and dice games and went on errands for the gamblers and bookmakers who treated me well with tips.

My normal optimism returned as I kept busy and I had money to spend. I began to think I found my future. Of course, this had to end. I came home one day as usual and found my mother sitting with a man I never knew existed, a New York City truant officer; she could not believe I missed the entire school term until she heard it from me. In my adolescent ignorance I thought no one but she would care, least of all the authorities. I was being given a summons to appear with her at Juvenile Court for a hearing. The judge explained I was not yet sixteen and it was against the law for me not to attend school. If I missed anymore school I would be sent to Reform School.

The next day, after solemn promises and tears, I arrived early enough at the school site and sat down in the concrete park across from the entrance. I watched students enter and envied the easy familiarity they had with each other and their sense of belonging there. But I could not get myself to follow them. I heard the bell ring and watched the door close, and with a strange combination of emptiness and freedom I stepped into a year long limbo.

CHAPTER THREE
The Formative Years

The unhappiness and despair I am sure I caused my parents were matched by my own confused feelings and sense of insecurity. My traditional cultural ties, with which I continued to maintain a most tenuous connection, held that an uneducated life was a waste. On some level I accepted those values and I knew dropping out of school was wrong for me. I did not think of my act as being sinful as when I consciously did something immoral, but it weighed heavily on my conscience and feeling of self-worth. I know well that feeling, as I also know that that knowledge is often seldom enough to prevent the act.

Because of my distance from my father, I did not realize how great a disappointment this was to him. My father's frustration was compounded by my return to the pool hall world he so despised. I later learned from one of his brothers that this was his world, too, when he was my age. He spent years shielding us from the details of his life to avoid the chance of our following him into it. Now, as all these efforts seemingly came to naught, he slipped into a fantasy which my mother abetted, if not shared—that he needed but "one big break and then he will put his boys into business." When my mother told me about these "plans" after his too-early death, I remember crying at the thought of how desperate I must have made him feel.

I was now sixteen, officially out of school with less than ten grades completed. My social skills were limited to a boy's world, even when I was with the men I spent much time with. If it were not for sex, girls need not exist. I suffered terrible erotic fantasies driven by seemingly out-of-control compulsions. It did not enhance my self-esteem to realize how powerless I was against these physiological forces, which I mistakenly believed were matters of will power. Since erotic fantasies are no basis for inter-gender relationships, I was painfully awkward with girls.

Needless to say, I was singularly unprepared for any meaningful life. A little older now, and without the constraints imposed by living the lie about attending school, I reentered that cynical, empty twilight world whose only purpose was "scoring." I worked at odd jobs to get money to gamble, and if lifelong gambling addicts cannot recognize their addiction, it should be no surprise that a sixteen-year-old did not recognize his. It was not winning or losing, I finally recognized many years later, but the "action" that counted; exactly like my father, I was always able to find money and never knew how to keep it.

For years, I thought of the unhappiness and conflicts of that time as stupid and self-inflicted behavior, a stubborn refusal or inability to heed the positive impulses trying to steer me in more constructive directions. I knew better but could not act better. I must again express wonder at my escape from the consequence of so many brainless, dangerous and destructive incidents I precipitated in those years. But what were apparently random events and decisions, when seen through a different prism can transform the meaning and dissolve the effects of those actions. It is in this sense the ideas of past lives and the effect of karma become so meaningful.

I do not say I "understand" these ideas. In India and other eastern cultures the concept of reincarnation and karma is absorbed at mother's knee in much the same way as learning one's native language. And like learning the language, the absorption of a cultural concept is less intellectual than visceral. For the adult, on the other hand, entering a new language and culture is a purely intellectual exercise, and it requires a long, difficult period for the person to learn to think in the language and feel in the culture. For me, this period of assimilation of the ideas of reincarnation and karma required little time and no rationalization.

I *feel* the validity of these notions grow as my spiritual practice progresses. Karma, the Sanskrit expression for the working out of ancient deeds, manifests in my conflicting compulsions with their strange resolutions; it emerges in repetitious suffering over time and again; and it surfaces with the continual fading of both the joy of accomplishment and the despair of failure; but above all, karma is seen most clearly at the instant of its demise, in its most subtle and ephemeral form, when one *knows* (not understands) its final bond has been severed not ever to be suffered again.

During this early period of my life, after dropping out of high school, I was living in an intellectual wasteland dominated by my sensory needs. But there was a part of me, sensing the nihilism of my life and given to introspection, that never ceased trying to break through. This interior disquiet was not clearly articulated and was mostly hidden, but it was shared with one boyhood friend who remained the flimsiest tie to my traditional community. After many attempts, he finally induced me to attend a lecture at the local YMHA, a branch of the city's Young Men's Hebrew Association. I do not know why I went then after resisting for so long; perhaps I simply wanted to please him. I had no feeling of ethnic alienation to keep me from going, if I had thought of that at all. Although, by now completely secular, I was not even bar mitzvahed as were my brothers, I continued my strong identification as part of the Jewish people.

So far as I remember, this was the first time I had ever entered that particular building. I do not remember the details of that lecture, but it is a safe assumption it had to do with the ongoing calamity of European Jewry. I came away galvanized by one of the speaker's ideas: in Hitler's mad attempt to eliminate the Jewish people, he made them the focus of world attention. Somehow that idea broke through my self-created insular shield and found a resonance with those inarticulate, disquieting longings. I went into the hall aware of the current intense anti-Semitism and the rise of Nazism, however, my response to these attitudes was as an individual; I dealt with them as a personal issue. But I walked out changed, connected in some way to a cohesive, worldwide, ancient people and through them to the world at large.

Placing the "Jewish Question" in the center of Western consciousness at that time, early 1939, was more prophetic, even though tragically so, than concrete. At that time, there was little general thought that the fate of these people mirrored the danger to the civilized world. Nor could I have known that the speaker's audience reflected in microcosm the thinking of European and American political, academic and intellectual circles.

I now entered an environment of ideas in which I found myself eerily at home. I had no intellectual structure or context in which to place or evaluate more than the simplest of these concepts, but I do not recall being cowed or disturbed by my inability to give them verbal meaning. Later, I thought of myself, in the ensuing days of that initial introduction to this new philosophical world, as the driest of deserts receiving the first seasonal rain calling its countless buried seeds to life and growth.

I began going to the "Y" on my own and fell into a small study group discussing world affairs. It was led by a City College student as part of a YMHA youth social program. Here I met Jewish refugees, mostly young German students who somehow escaped Nazi Germany, and Zionist youth who were training and preparing to live in Palestine. There were the full complement of Marxist movements with their endless theoretical debates and niggling differences. Before long, I had a new vocabulary, a new set of friends and a new perspective. I did not break away from my old habits or haunts. But these daily activities became moderated by my evening ones. With more and more confidence, I participated in the ubiquitous political discussions, trying out every new idea I heard or read. Without going anywhere, I reached a new world.

Although I was not yet part of any organized political group, I now considered myself a socialist in its broadest sense, believing that a new economic system should replace the present, clearly defunct, capitalist economy. In my new enthusiasm, I began talking like this everywhere, including at home. My mother could not often follow my newly minted logic, not surprisingly, but she appreciated my less surly and more open personality. For the first time in many years, I could talk to her about what I was thinking, what I was interested in, and what I was doing without evading her questions, lying, or sneaking out on her. I also got my father's attention.

He knew and disapproved of how I was spending my time since I stopped going to school. I can only speculate why he never confronted me with that disapproval, but it is not unlikely that as long as he could pretend he did not know, he did not have to confront his inability to do anything about it. If that was, indeed, the case, it did not apply to his willingness to take a stand against my political ideas. I became, in his words, a "flaming communist." I tried to talk with him about my ideas, but talk between us was so mutually alien that it was impossible. He accused me of things I had never heard of and I never would have thought he knew about: I was a subversive, my "communist" friends robbed banks to finance their revolution, I was running around with girls who believed in "free love," and he, futilely, forbade me to go to the "Y" again. I could not understand his rage and unreasonableness. What was a glimmer of light for me on one side of my life, giving me, finally, a sense of purpose, made the other side, our relationship, even darker.

In due course, I met the person who would steer the course for the next ten years of my life and, incidentally, provide the material and philosophical anchor for much of the rest of it. Marshal B. was a young college student, a few years my senior in age but a generation ahead in intellect and knowledge. He was the first person I knew I could call a scholar, although I would not have known that word then. He was the son of Russian-Jewish immigrants and, perhaps not strangely considering our relationship, I would not know anything more about his personal life. Besides speaking an academic English, he was fluent in Russian, German and Yiddish at least. He frequented the "Y" but I do not remember him before we met.

In one of the never-ending political debates, which I now attended regularly, I asked a question of one of the speakers. Later, after the meeting, Marshal came up to me, introduced himself, commended me on my question and began to discuss it with me. He spoke to my mind in such a way that captured my heart. There was no condescension on his part, and I sensed an intelligence and range of knowledge I did not think I had previously encountered. Before we parted that evening, he lent me a little paper bound book to read. *The Communist Manifesto*, by Karl Marx and Frederick Engels, published in 1848, was the first Marxist political tract, and the first one I ever read. It was also the token that meant we would meet again.

For the next several months my attention revolved around those meetings. Two or three evenings a week we would go off by ourselves to discuss—less discussion than elucidation by him of the ideas contained in an overflowing well of reading material he supplied. There was no such thing as an isolated intellectual concept; every idea was illustrated by reference to history, politics, philosophy, economics, psychology and their sub-texts. A skeleton was created out of words and names: dialectical and historical materialism, idealism, political economy, capitalism and socialism, class struggle, and a pantheon of ancient and modern thinkers. And layer by layer that skeleton acquired the flesh and blood and sinew of a philosophical system and worldview that answered all questions and solved all problems.

I think differently of this period now than I did then. I look back in awe of the mysterious nature of the person absorbing this knowledge. Absorption is truly the word, for it was not a function of intellect. It was necessary only to hear, to read and to define in order to understand. I would read at night in my shared bedroom, under a tent-like blanket with flashlight and dictionary, teasing out the meaning word by word and sentence by sentence of the most esoteric thoughts. Even now I can remember typical Engelian Zen-like koans that I would mull over and over in my mind until their meaning would reveal itself in a flash like the newly created bit of matter in a particle collider.

It never occurred to me then that there was anything unusual taking place. This was only one aspect of my life, and if other changes took place, as they did, the connections were not obvious. But the intellectual change was monumental, even though it seemed without any immediate impact on my life and activity. I entered my seventeenth year ignorant of humanity's most rudimentary intellectual accomplishments, and left it able to move comfortably among some of its most exquisite thought. Years later, its mystery and clarification converged simultaneously in Socrates' explication of the ever recurring human query, "who are we?"

> Then, since the soul is immortal and often born, having seen what is on earth and what is in the house of Hades, and everything, there is nothing it has not learnt; so

> there is no wonder it can remember about virtue and
> other things, because it knew about these before. For
> since all nature is akin, and the soul has learnt every-
> thing, there is nothing to hinder a man, remembering
> one thing only—which men call learning—from himself
> finding out all else, if he is brave and does not weary in
> seeking; for seeking and learning is all remembrance.[1]

The full range of one's motives are often shrouded, but in my
friend's case it became clear he was steering my interest toward
Marxism and Communism—and specifically, the Young Communist League (YCL)— a youth adjunct of the Communist Party. But
in his defense, if any defense is needed, no one was more ready or
willing to enter that community than I was. Moreover, if it were
simply community I wanted, I had other options that may have
appeared more attractive, and certainly more respectable. But
desire for entrance into that world arose with knowledge of it.
Because I was not yet eighteen, I could not formally join the YCL,
but I was introduced to members and attended meetings on an
informal basis.

After I became a "card carrying" member of the YCL, Marshal
disappeared from my life for about six years. Our loss of contact
seemed quite normal and I do not remember missing it. Many years
later, sparked by a relationship with another friend (a more clearly
spiritual mentor), I noticed the similarity of these two associations
and then recalled other times when people, in person or through
other types of contact, touched my life, changed it, and then disappeared.

I met Marshal briefly once again, after World War II when we
had both returned from Europe. His service as a Special Services
officer brought him into contact with the Soviet Army, Soviet
Communism and "the new Communist man." His disillusionment
was total. But for me, everything I had seen in that European catas-
trophe only reinforced my Marxist convictions. The one thing I

remember most about this last meeting was the quality of my feeling toward him. Until then, he remained in my mind as an intellectual model, almost an icon. But that former awe was gone. We talked, we understood similar events differently, we parted. What he had to give me in those intoxicating early days I wanted and needed and was starving for. Now this new knowledge, from the very same source, perhaps as important and valid, fell on those deafest of ears, the ones that refuse to hear.

My life's situation reversed completely in its psychological and material dimensions. Before I was living a purposeless existence trying to satisfy gross sensory needs, and denying obscure and contradictory, albeit more positive impulses. Now, those positive impulses emerged full blown in my consciousness, overshadowing the previously dominant ones. The attractions of my former life stayed with me nonetheless for many years and were often times indulged. In fact, the chief conflict in my existence, and a great source of suffering and self-deprecation, was my difficulty in controlling these passions. My inability in this area made my appreciation of the power of spiritual practice even greater as I witnessed the effortless loosening of this sensory, and sensual, domination.

Marxism, Marx taught, is the first philosophical system that wanted not only to explain the world, but also to transform it. Capitalism, he pointed out, made this transformation possible, and inevitable, by its economic organization of the working class; and now fascism made it imminent by revealing its true nature for all to see. It was only necessary to open the eyes of the masses by giving direction and organization to their natural struggle for livable working conditions and productive lives.

This was possible on the basis of the inexhaustible wealth created by labor and now appropriated by nonproducers, i.e. capitalists. Society can be restructured to provide an ever-rising standard of living, satisfying the needs of its least resourceful members and providing incentives for the contributions of its most ambitious. Moreover, this ancient utopian dream was now within humankind's grasp because of the theoretical genius of Marx and Engels, the organizational genius of Lenin, and now the leadership genius of Stalin. I am well aware that, from the point of view of many post-World War II Americans, these ideas could have had validity only in the irrational mind of a naive seventeen-year old; but, I would suggest, even now, that point of view misses the significance of much twentieth-century history.

Before the end of the year, I started my first regular job and remained never more than a semiprofessional wage earner for the following fifty years. But for the next twelve years, what work I did was secondary to my efforts propagandizing and organizing for socialism. Wherever I worked, I tried out my new-found ideas and early learned how strange, and in many cases threatening, they were to those who theoretically should have been the most receptive. Even in the most natural form of working class organization, the labor union, many workers were resistant and fearful; cowed by employer and often by their religious leaders, not to mention police and civic authorities, it required heroic and special leadership qualities to overcome those fears and defy the antilabor threats and violence that generated them.

I had no special leadership ability nor, to be sure, heroic qualities. Not then at eighteen nor later in my maturity. But I had a strong sense of responsibility and commitment that came from some mysterious source. In addition, my recently discovered ability to understand and explain the often obscure doctrines that directed our comradely lives generated a respect and appreciation I had never had and I greatly valued. Explanations, I also learned shortly, did not have to be "true," they only had to explain. This ability was of great importance in that period of the

German/USSR nonaggression treaty, a time that created so much confusion and despair in the worldwide anti-fascist movement.

I soon assumed leadership of our local YCL branch. This was more by default than ability, but I began to romanticize myself as an aspiring revolutionary. Branch activity consisted of regular discussion and planning meetings. Leaflet distribution around current issues was an important "propaganda and agitation" activity, as was the distribution and sale of the Party newspaper, the *Sunday Worker*. As branch leader, I routinely met with "comrades" on higher YCL levels who were normally regular Communist Party members. My ideological connections to the world Communist and anti-fascist movements was more and more cemented by this physical connection.

My life at home changed dramatically. I was making a steady financial contribution and this was no small matter. But my focus fell completely outside my personal family, as I acquired a new family that satisfied deep emotional, intellectual and fraternal needs. But this was not membership in a fraternal organization. For all the professed atheism of the world Marxist movement, few religions could boast more devoted adherence. I felt part of a nurturing community. More experienced and leading comrades guided my political "education" with study sessions and seminars, and they steered me toward more formal courses on Labor History, Political Science, Economics and Philosophy at a local community college. More than that, I established the closest personal ties I had up to then experienced with a diverse population that cut across every ethnic group.

I achieved an independence from my parents that I later realized was unprecedented among my peers and siblings, but which, of course, I took for granted. I was at home only to sleep. My father and I avoided each other, and my mother was painfully ambivalent about my activities, of which she had only a vague idea. On the one hand, she perceived a purpose and happiness in my life that she could only applaud, but on the other, she still regarded me as an immature eighteen-year-old who was being beguiled and used by incomprehensible forces. Later, she told me, as frightened and worried as she was when I prepared to embark for Europe during World War II, she was often as frightened and worried at my earlier political activities.

These political activities consumed my life. I volunteered for everything. Demonstrations, protests, union organizing, street corner meetings. Every Sunday I was up early to arrange for *Worker* distribution, and more often than not I was the only branch member present despite previous assurances by others that they would be there. But no matter, I learned my lessons well and knew socialist victory was an historical necessity. By word and deed, I believed these ideas would be infused into the minds of the masses until, as Marx taught, they became an irresistible material force.

I was sustained and inspired by the persuasiveness of the philosophy, the beauty of the goals and the never-ending stories of heroic men and women comrades fighting for these same ideals in all countries. I had older friends and mentors who had imbibed these ideas with their mother's milk. New York had its share of European immigrant veterans of continental and Russian revolutionary struggles, and I was regaled with stories of the leaders of these movements, and ordinary "worker-heroes" by old-time party members who had personally experienced these events.

Above all, did we not have the living proof of the viability of this vision in Stalin's Soviet Union? But even then, the dream was dead, killed as it was being born, by an unbridled paranoia and growing madness. There were rumors and whispers of excesses and betrayals, but who would believe these stories, spread as they were by "capitalist lackeys." Anti-Soviet ideas were pernicious thoughts after all, and refuting an intellectual thought is simply a matter of superior logic; destroying a dream, however, is not that easy.

How many brave men and women, within and outside of Soviet Russia, went to their deaths believing their socialist dream was intact and protected by the man who had tortured and killed it at least a decade earlier. Perversely, this betrayal was first silenced and then hidden by the German invasion of the Soviet Union. Stalin wove together for the Soviet people and the world the defense of the Soviet Communist system with the necessity of the anti-Nazi war. To say the least, these ideas were not part of the thinking of most Americans. But in Europe they motivated, inspired and organized the internal resistance to Nazi occupiers.

By early 1942 all these political questions were muted. I was working in upstate New York in a steel mill as a small part of the effort to organize steel workers into the CIO United Steel Workers union. There was plenty of wartime work and young people were entering the mills from small towns and farms. It was thought I could be of some help in that drive. For me, it meant a chance to work with the "industrial working class" who were the heart of the revolutionary proletariat. In addition, for the first time I would be isolated from any support structure, family or friends, because I was going into an area where there was a pervasive anti-socialist, anti-union atmosphere.

The steel mill made high-grade tool steel by melting down scrap metal and special ores in large electric ovens. I was part of a seven-man crew that loaded the ovens using a long steel peel. Three of us were on each side and the crew chief would guide the peel, the pan edge loaded with the material to be melted down, into the part of the oven it was needed. It was hard work but I enjoyed the physicality of it and the work gave me a strong sense of satisfaction.

My role was to work with the influx of new workers coming into industrial work from the surrounding rural areas. These mostly young people had little exposure to trade unionism and, like the American worker in general, no sense of themselves as an economic class. In the end, the mill did vote to join the union I was there to promote and I like to think I had a place, even if small, in that victory. It was, however, a difficult time both in external activity and internal conflicts.

Like me, many of these young people were without family and community restraints for the first time. Although my primary purpose for being there was to instill in them the ideals of trade unionism and "class consciousness," their new freedom and interests centered in another direction. Freedom meant drinking, gambling and girls, and now that they had money they lost little time satisfying those desires. As I made friends and socialized with them, I easily rationalized that I fell in with them and their activities to win their confidence and attention. But that innate disposition toward my former lifestyle, which I had thought I long ago left behind, likely explains this lapse more accurately.

This was not the last time I lost my focus, and each time it would be accompanied by confusion and guilt, and a loss of a sense of worth. I realize now these "falls" were expressions of conflicting forces in my being, and I had not the willpower to overcome them. The fact that I was twenty years old could mitigate some of the self-blame at that time, but that only made it worse as I recognized these same faults as I got older. All too often, doing the right or wrong thing was a function less of the circumstances in which I found myself and more of emotional and physiological drives I could not subdue, not withstanding a seemingly strong, principled, intellectual core.

For the next six months I led an unfocused, carousing life, easily dissuaded from attempts to talk of matters I was supposed to discuss such as worker organization or unions. Finally, reality set in with a notice to report and register for the draft. I did not want to enter the military from upstate so I returned home. The timing could not have been better. A day after returning, I had an attack of acute appendicitis that required immediate surgery. I was told the appendix was ready to burst. I do not know what would have been the outcome if I were still in Syracuse without any support or resources.

This incident represents another example of that recurring occult pattern in my life I now see so clearly. Over and over, through ignorance or character flaws, I would find myself in a potentially destructive personal situation, only to see that situation somehow dissolve without subsequent negative consequences. Then, of course, the thought of karma or spiritual guidance did not exist. But now these ideas offer exquisite insights into other areas of my life where I was unable to translate whatever intelligence or ability I had into more than a continuous struggle to maintain a marginal economic status. The surface side of my life during its householder and child-raising period was so beset by economic problems that its potential quality was never realized. Blindly, I reacted to each crisis as a singular event without a clue about its universal connections.

In this context my surgery had its positive side. I decided to enlist in the military rather than be drafted. Because of my recent operation, I could not immediately go on active service so my recruiting advisor suggested I enlist in the Signal Corps Reserves and attend school for Radio Operator's training. This three-month period would permit full recuperation and provide me with an Army skill classification. I would then enter the Army in a specific branch, the Signal Corps, with a classified skill that would likely keep me out of the general replacement pool.

In my fantasies, I saw myself as a combat soldier fighting on the front lines of the anti-fascist war. Actually, I made unsuccessful efforts to realize these notions. But this classification made it unlikely I would see that aspect of the war. Later, I came to understand how fortunate I was not to have to endure that test. I suffered enemy bombings and artillery fire. In one three-month period, on the Anzio beachhead in Italy, I was subject to sustained enemy action as part of the support effort. Often, I was close enough to the front lines to see infantry troops just as they were relieved for rest and I had a sense of what they encountered. Nothing I experienced equaled what those men had to face.

My decision to enlist met with resistance at home. I needed parental permission to do so since I was not yet twenty-one. My father and I had by then reached a reconciliation of sorts because, I am sure, the imminence of my going away to war put our differences into a reasonable perspective. His was a much better understanding of the reality, seriousness and danger of actual warfare than my romantic visions. He finally and reluctantly agreed not to stand in my way, but he would not sign the application papers; it was my mother who had to. Years later, she told me he was afraid to sign out of a superstitious fear he would bring me bad luck. In any case, from the time I entered active service he wrote me a letter every day, if only a few lines, even when ill, and even those days when my mother would write.

For me, entering the military was a continuation of my personal commitment to the defeat of fascism and the struggle for socialism. I was conscious of being part of an historic, decisive world conflict between progressive and reactionary forces, and I was sure the end of the war would realize humanity's highest social aspirations. Perhaps for this reason, I did not think of my years of service as wasted, nor as an interruption of other more important activities. Needless to say, there was little encouragement for that point of view in the Army, which was maintaining morale on the basis of defending the "American way of life" and spreading it throughout the world.

But once overseas—we landed in Naples, Italy from North Africa soon after Italy surrendered, but with the German Army in fact occupying that country—I found that what were isolated intellectual ideas in an American context were generally accepted and little challenged in Europe. But at this point, these political differences were silenced, co-opted by the U.S., USSR, British alliance, with its main focus on unconditionally destroying the German Nazi system. As the war ended with Europe in ruins: tens of millions dead, millions more displaced, homeless, scattered without family, indeed without country— the extent of the absolute evil nature of fascism was finally revealed when the concentration camps were discovered.

The prestige of the Soviet Union and the Red Army was at its zenith, and from my perspective it seemed clear that socialist ideals, led by communists in Italy and France and less radical forces in Great Britain, were accepted as the rewards of the people's victory and for their historic suffering. My intellectual ideas were vindicated without question, but surprisingly, I could not feel a corresponding emotional satisfaction. I began to sense an isolation from the historic events taking place. The American Communist Party had dissolved during the war to become an "association." From an orthodox Marxist perspective, this was the same as renouncing socialism and the class struggle.

My feelings were ambivalent at the time I heard that news. I could not understand the idea from a theoretical level, but simultaneously I felt a sense of freedom. For the first time, I comprehended the psychological burden the intellectual restraints of Party discipline and the Party line imposed. Those missionary impulses that diminished my sense of individuality in favor of the collective were no longer burning so brightly. But then, these negative notions were still only mental whispers eclipsed by the evidence everywhere in Europe, and in front of my eyes, especially through my personal contact with the Italian people, of the mass demand for a new progressive social order.

I returned home to a different America, one on the verge of its greatest period of prosperity. On a fundamental level, I changed much less than my wartime experiences would have warranted. On the surface, my military experience provided a fully mature appreciation of personal independence. I expected to live physically apart from my family and make independent work and social decisions. But despite this, without the discipline and focus of my former political activities, I found myself directionless. I joined my parents in Florida, where my father was trying a last unsuccessful attempt to exploit the pent-up wealth accumulated during the war. That short visit revealed an emptiness I had not felt since the day I left school almost ten years ago. Despite the justifiable national optimism, I found myself without purpose or interest.

In early 1946, I returned to New York and made contact with former comrades who were reconstituting and rebuilding the Communist Party. This was done more out of default than conviction. What I had missed and tried to regain from this new commitment was the positive enthusiasm, the revolutionary fervor, of those earlier years. I know now, but could never then envision, that those former emotions originated in, yet were a poor substitute for, the desire and contact with a transcendent spiritual self buried deep within me. Predictably, the next four years were spiritless, often confused and unproductive. In addition, and most importantly, I had married during this period, and with this new focus I began to think of ending my Party connections and the activities for which I was still responsible.

I felt guilty about these attitudes and considered them personal failings, but I soon learned these feelings were not peculiar to me.

In an important way, they reflected the times. The Party became more and more isolated, not only by the general public, where at best it had had little support, but also in intellectual circles and the labor movement where it lost out in many formerly supportive unions. Finally, because of a large membership loss, the trial and imprisonment of its leadership, and the developing anti-Communist hysteria, the Party turned inward and went "underground." Marginal people were simply ignored and cast adrift. Without resistance on my part, and with a sense of liberation and relief, I became one of those.

I entered the Communist movement at age seventeen and now, at age twenty-eight, we parted company. It is impossible to know what alternative decisions would have led to in those early adolescent days. But I recognized in those years, and I feel confirmed in that recognition now, an emergence and maturing of a vital intellectual center. The positive internationalist, humanistic outlook that developed then and remains today is one I treasure for the sustenance it provided and provides yet.

If equanimity and emotional balance are hallmarks of a growing spiritual life, progressive socialist compassion balanced with the ideals of individual democratic freedom could well be an equivalent marker for a balanced social life. Marxist Socialist thinking remained a constructive intellectual force in my life, but not until gaining the insights afforded by my spiritual experience did I realize its essential fallacy: it is not changing the world that will change man, as Marxist materialism holds; rather changing man will change the world, as spiritual transformation in the final years of the twentieth century is proving more and more.

Chapter Four

The Preparatory Years

I *have mentioned several examples of how spiritual practice opens new windows into interior understanding.* Only intuition, not rational thought, reveals the mysterious attraction between disparate individuals that both binds them and provides mutual support and growth. This new insight surfaced with a special clarity after marriage, however, as my wife and family became the center of a different focus. My spiritual map reveals how the primitive road of my formative years spilled out onto the beginning of a broad two-lane highway leading to unimagined opportunities. Although the two lanes enjoyed interchangeable access, they were not similarly paved: one was relatively smooth with easily seen rewards; the other, bumpy, filled with potholes, detours, barriers and frustrating switchbacks. Both sides of my life had to be traversed to their ends before they merged into one smooth, superhighway.

We were married for a year before I got my first job capable of providing a stable living for us. Driving a bread truck as a route salesman for a fairly large commercial bakery marked the beginning of a definitive time in our lives. Even though I earned a moderate income, I was forced to work extra jobs, work on my days off and work during my vacation period when possible. This economic condition remained a salient feature of our lives for many years, and then, when it seemed we were finally in a secure situation, I was again thrown back into a marginal financial status.

Strangely however, despite all my demonstrably unwise and

unjustifiable actions, at least in the eyes of wiser and more successful "advisors," our most important life decisions proved the correct ones. In fact, even what was looked upon as economic failure, and what I thought of as economic inadequacy, provided us with a satisfying lifestyle and made it possible for our children to get a fine primary and secondary education. It is only now, from the vantage point of its virtual completion, that I understand the general positive evolutionary nature of this entire period, a completely opposite perception from the one I had when living through it.

Three of our seven children were born within the first five years of our marriage. This, of course, established the basic structure of our lives for the following two decades or more; I was primarily responsible for our financial needs and Florence was the center of our home and family life. It is astonishing that she was able to do so much with the meager resources I supplied. Despite this inadequacy, it is to her credit that we were able to provide a secure and stable environment for our children. In this, on the surface at least, we were not too much different from other successful families of our time.

But if we looked like other families from the outside, our internal family situation began early to assume the nonconformist perspectives and behavior that would always characterize it. Many years earlier, I had been introduced to the concept of natural living with its back-to-nature ideas of nutrition and natural healing. I was intrigued and well-disposed toward these ideas, but my socialist interests and beliefs did not accommodate a serious consideration of them. When I was once again introduced to these views, primarily through the writing of J. I. Rodale who was just beginning to publish his rediscovery of ancient perennial organic farming and natural health theories, they struck me with a new force and conviction.

Almost immediately, Florence and I began to incorporate these concepts into our family life. Whole grains, natural foods, and the few nutritional supplements that were available, became part of our daily regimen. Organic farming had a special appeal, and although we were living in a three-story walkup in Ossining N.Y., we were able to borrow a little garden plot from a neighbor to grow a few vegetables. This back-to-land desire was much less mysterious to Florence, who grew up on a farm, than it was to my city-bred nature. Not so slowly, we started to transform our material lives deliberately, and, unconsciously, our spiritual lives.

This goal of good physical health, freedom from illness and its fears, and the desire for a general sense of well-being is a universal one. I am again reminded, as I write these words, that those worthy goals, which we looked for as ends in themselves, are in reality, "side effects" of spiritual growth. I could not have thought then that these positive feelings were in any way akin to those of my early idealistic days. But now I recognize that all positive, uplifting, life-supporting impulses represent the soul's attempt to forge its way into human awareness, oftentimes through a heavily clogged vehicle.

Once again, my life was lifted out of the narrow focus of my own immediate needs as I began to identify with larger "cosmic purposes." Despite our marginal resources we began to explore the possibilities of finding an environment to support this more natural way of living. It soon became clear our dream of a small house on a small parcel of land, an eloquent echo of John Steinbeck's characters in his classic book, *Of Mice and Men*, was impossible in the area in which we were then living. Nevertheless, we continued looking for what we increasingly thought of as a miracle. The answer to this prayer came one day as we noticed an advertisement for building lots and small houses opening up in a southern Connecticut village. According to the developer, we could finance the lot and then use the paid-up lot as a down payment for a house he would build on it. Although it represented a long, hard commute to my work, and it was a small, isolated community, especially since Florence would be without a car, we made an instant decision to buy it.

No decision was more important and fruitful as the one we made in that instant. Now, after forty years, we are still enjoying its fruits. In many ways, that decision was the first solid step on that smooth road I spoke of earlier. The developer, William W., took our last $875 as a down payment on the lot, and we financed the remaining $1000. Within a year, working every extra hour I could, and consumed by the approaching realization of our dream, we paid off the lot loan. True to his word, Mr. W. guided us through the mortgage proceedings, and secured a bank loan for building. He accepted a noninterest note for $500 to make us eligible for bank financing. By August, 1957, about a year from the time we first saw his advertisement, we were in our own home. This was about eight weeks before our fourth child was born.

This fateful move established the foundation of the physical structure of our family union and made it possible, as I will explain, for us to live productive lives, and for our children to receive benefits far beyond what could be expected from a surface examination of our monetary means. Without forethought, and despite every failed and anxiety-ridden attempt on my part to bring an end to our continuous money shortage, it turned out that this inability to earn more than a marginal income for many years was the key to our successful future. Understanding this then was impossible, of course, and I suffered terribly over my lack of ability to improve that situation.

Mr. W. played a central role in this future for the short time he was involved in it. We unwittingly put ourselves and our scarce resources in his hands, to exploit either for his own purposes or to satisfy our needs. Had we known of his reputation in this town we may never have had made this decision. We learned too late that he was a disbarred lawyer and a very shady real estate dealer. Almost without exception, the people who had had dealings with him found their relationship frustrating, verging often on illegality and marked by corner-cutting and broken promises. More than a few needed court action, and we found none with a good word for him. But in our lives he was a willing accomplice to those powerful positive forces Florence and I must have accumulated over the eons.

There are those who congratulated us on our "luck," and we had accepted that dry and empty rationalization. But a better explanation for our apparent good "luck" came to me many years later when reading Maharishi Mahesh Yogi's book *Science of Being and Art of Living*. The following long quote is justified, I believe, because of its direct relevance to this situation.

> None other than himself is responsible for a man's happiness or suffering. If a man enjoys, he enjoys out of his own doings; if a man suffers, he suffers out of his own doings.
>
> If a man—call him Mr. X [my Mr. W.]—comes to us and is very happy and good-natured and brings us much joy, we think he is nothing but a bundle of happiness. But the philosophy of karma says that Mr. X is only a bundle of happiness to you because he is at that time delivering to you the happiness that you once spread in the world. The reaction of your good karma is coming through him...Had Mr. X actually been a bundle of happiness, then he would not be an unhappy companion to some others on some other side of his life.[1]

Although we felt intuitively that we were doing the best for ourselves, in our most optimistic moods we could not have imagined how well we were actually to be situated. Our physical location turned out to be ideal. We had only a one-quarter acre lot but to our immediate rear were tens of acres of forested lands that became conservancy open space never to be touched or developed. One side was a large open lot to which we had access and later were able to buy. For many years we satisfied our homesteading desires with a large organic garden, and at one point we kept chickens and bees for eggs and honey. It was a quiet, semirural area only minutes from town and remains such to this day.

But as well provided as we were on this level, we also, again without conscious thought or planning, moved into a young, upper class, growing community with a strong motivation toward providing children with the best possible public education. We moved in as the town entered a steep growing cycle, requiring the building of virtually a new school system that was to be the focus of community activity for years to come. This system, which remains a model for my state of Connecticut, provided our children with an exceptional educational foundation making it possible for all of them to move on to higher education.

Both Florence and I were acutely aware, right from the start of our new life here, of its potential blessings. But as promising and fulfilling as it was, maintaining and providing for it proved a never-ending struggle. In truth, I was not a good route salesman. We worked on a base pay plus commission, and I seldom earned more than my base pay. I was unmotivated and disliked my work and felt trapped because of my family needs. It was only the satisfaction of those needs that made the work bearable.

It was not an easy life. I awoke early in the morning to get to work by four or earlier, and this was after an almost one hour commute. Whenever I could, I worked an extra day, and for many years I took vacation pay in lieu of a vacation. It was common for me to leave my house at three in the morning not to return until three or later in the afternoon. For one prolonged period I was delivering newspapers after my regular day's work. Rushing to this second job meant neglecting my primary one, which resulted in creating new problems for myself. No matter what I did, however, it seemed we never had enough money. I was more than once chided by my mother and siblings who saw this lack as proof of failure. I must confess it was a source of self-doubt, even as I tried to justify our lifestyle by its obvious benefits.

It was equally difficult for Florence. We had four small children when we moved to our new home, and then three more before the end of the next decade. It was a heroic challenge. Clothing was sewn, resewn, refitted with few new items. For years we did not see a movie or eat a dinner out. If I remember correctly, she got a fully automatic washing machine before I got my first new car, but both these celebratory milestones came only after years of toil. This account, however, of harshness and struggle is a distorted and incomplete picture; one colored by the conventional American measure of success—the accumulation of material wealth. But I sensed then, and I know now, that that standard is a false one.

Our internal family structure was strong, focused and disciplined. Our early commitment to natural living, which translated into healthful, holistic fresh food, fresh air and exercise, was easily encouraged and practiced in this environment. There were two or three nearby farms, one of them organic, where fresh whole milk was available. Nutritional supplements seriously challenged our budget, but we found money for them. In the summer and fall we had fresh garden produce, and we learned how to preserve much of it.

From the very beginning, our children were guided by two explicit directives: the importance of good health and good educa-tion. The implicit values of love, respect and unforced consideration of others were so much a part of their mother's nature they could not help but imbibe them. Over the years neighbors and others regularly complimented us for the behavior of our children.

I did not think then in terms of the realization of a vision, or the materialization of an aspect of the American Dream. If these family accomplishments indicated that this was, indeed, the case, it was hidden by the failures and difficulties in the other equally important facets of my life that did not permit its full savor. I came to marriage and parenthood grossly unprepared for either of them. My lack of formal education was an obvious disadvantage, and I had had no work experience outside of factory work. My job as a route salesman was a step above a delivery man's. Although, it was true, in this job as in almost any, there were opportunities for growth and promotion, I made no effort and showed little interest in pursuing them. This failing was despite my acute awareness I had no skills and otherwise little economic future. For whatever reason, I could not find the emotional or psychological resources to give the necessary attention to make my work fruitful.

Rather than change my attitude toward my job, which one would think was the only reasonable response, I decided that I would study radio and television repair with the idea of learning a trade and perhaps starting a small household repair business. I made this decision at the beginning of the television age in American life when service people seemed to be as important as doctors. The promises of the correspondence school's advertisements beguiled me, and I eagerly accepted their stated record of success in training students. I only learned much later how much overstated that record actually was; in fact, less than five percent of enrolled students completed their course of study and went on to achieve positions in the field. I enrolled in the school. Besides theoretical knowledge, it offered hands-on training working with parts and instruments that had to be purchased through the school. Somehow, we always managed to find tuition and payment for these needed items. I see clearly now that I put myself into an impossible situation through my own willful stupidity and jeopardized the well-being and future of my family. I perversely refused to concentrate my attention on the work that was supporting all of us, doing just the barest minimum to hold my job, and now deliberately finding a reason not to change that destructive behavior. I was holding out to myself and to Florence, as a real prospect, the chimerical possibility of converting what was in reality apprenticeship training, even if completed, into a job supporting her and four children. But this fateful life decision, like the others before it, proved correct although certainly it was not a rational act.

I gave all my attention to school work. Despite my woefully inadequate background in mathematics, I was always able to master the elements I needed for my work. When I first saw the basic math formulae required by this new study I realized I had no foundation for them. However, students were assured that understanding this level of theory was not necessary for accomplishing their study goals. I knew intuitively, though, that without it one would remain on a very low level of ability.

I remember my first tentative steps in unraveling these mysteries. And I remember the surge of confidence I felt when with this even very elementary knowledge I was able to design simple electronic circuits and predict electronic reaction. Simple as these beginnings were, I felt I was moving in the right direction.

In time, perhaps a year after starting this training, I started to repair TV sets on a part-time basis. My goal of operating a repair business out of my house was an impractical and unrealizable one for many reasons, not the least of which was I had no resources, but it colored my thinking. The idea of quitting my bakery job, and my continuing perfunctory attitude toward it precipitated a crisis situation. I was doing the absolute minimum at work, and I entered an inexcusable, self-inflicted demoralized state which I thought I could not reverse even if I wanted to.

Florence knew I wanted to leave my job, but she had no idea of my situation at work. My fantasy was demonstrably irrational, and I knew I could not justify it. She saw my position, rightly, as the basis for family security, not only for the necessary pay check, which was becoming more and more adequate, but also for the health and insurance benefits provided by contract. She had a right to be uneasy of my increasing talk of finding a new job and starting over somewhere else. Yet she was prepared to support whatever decision I made, and that moral and emotional support, the confidence and faith in me that it indicated, made everything else possible.

I had by then gained some little background in industrial electronics—how very little I was soon to learn—and I began a tentative search for a place in the many new electronic plants opening in our area. Clearly my present employer was not being fairly served by my attitude and work, and as clearly, I did not deserve any rewards for my actions. And yet, with perfect timing, I once again escaped my negative activity without penalty and found my fantasy plans fulfilled. Just as my regular job was reaching a disastrous climax, I found an entry-level position in the electronics industry.

To get my new job, which was in response to a newspaper advertisement, I had to pass an application test in basic electronic theory as an absolute minimum. Aside from that, I was completely unqualified for the position. My schooling was questionable, especially compared to other applicants who were mainly young technical school graduates from accredited trade schools. My previous nine years as a route salesman was hardly equivalent experience. I "exaggerated" my television repair activities, which as it turned out mattered little, as it had no relevance for the proto-type development department in which I was placed.

Almost all of us who applied, I found out later, were hired, and my qualifications or lack of them played a minor role in the decision to hire me. It was enough, it appeared in those days, to know the difference between a vacuum tube and a light bulb. There was a virtual explosion in the newly created electronics industry of the late 1950s and early 1960s, fueled by the USSR's Sputnik orbiter, the creation of the United States' National Aeronautics and Space Administration (NASA) and President Kennedy's later proposal to land a man on the moon before the end of the '60s.

What I had inadvertently done was catch a ride on the express train of the new industrial age, just as it was departing the station. The decision to study electronics approximately eighteen months earlier was made in absolute ignorance of those potential developments. But that decision was the genesis for the reversal from a self-imposed, destructive path of action to a creative, life-supporting one. That pattern, then invisible, was so clear now, where over and over I would recklessly dive into a churning ocean, learning nothing from my mistakes, only to be rescued at the last moment.

The next three years were not without their difficulties, but these were the problems of growth, not the deterioration I had experienced earlier. My experience repairing TV sets, minimal at best, was completely inadequate for the quality of work in this industry, all of which had to meet high levels of military standards. I was hired to wire assembly prototype units, and I never learned to properly wire or solder. My supervisor took one look at my work and forbade me ever to pick up a soldering iron again. To ensure that, he promoted me to test and inspection duties.

This was a period of "being in the flow." There was no logical reason why I was moved from a situation where I could not do anything right to one into which I could not do anything wrong, but I have long given up on logic as a tool for understanding life, especially my own. I was first assigned to test finished units and components and then later I was moved into troubling-shooting defective units. I was now immersed in a new environment, surrounded by engineers and technicians, on the threshold of the new industrial revolution with the first, hesitant introduction of semiconductor technology. Although the full ramifications of those discoveries could not be known then, nothing else was talked of or was of interest—an early indication of the scope of these changes.

Being at work was like being in school, and there was no lack of willing teachers. It soon became apparent to me that the one-pointed effort I earlier put into the understanding of basic electronic theory, to the detriment of my other work at the time, formed a solid foundation on which to build a professional, or at the least, a semiprofessional career. I was not mistaken. Finally, my working life was rising to the positive level of my family environment. The two lanes of my life's highway were coming together in a long smooth stretch.

By 1962, after three years of intensive work and study, my first tentative steps into this new industry became a solid footing of knowledge and experience. I considered myself a skilled technician and was so considered by my now second electronics employer. Work was a continuous learning experience and study was simply a means to understand work. My present work situation was a day-and-night contrast with my previous employment only a few short years ago in terms of interest, attention, morale and future anticipation.

My ability to reach this level of competence in my work and my solid theoretical foundation for growth was a source of satisfaction and pride. My fears ended that I would fail my family from lack of training or ability. I knew I was in a growing industry, and I was confident I could master the technical skills necessary to grow with it. What I did not know, however, was that these intellectual skills were only a part, and, indeed, not the most important part, of the balanced personality needed for success in life. For the first time, I began to understand there were other areas of my life, not simply deficient work skills, that undermined my chances for achievement.

Because of these deficiencies, I was now unhappily preparing to leave a job I took two years earlier, without realizing its potential. To be sure, my hands-on technical skills and the theoretical basis for their improvement were continually growing, as I found little difficulty with study and understanding. Ironically, however, I finally realized that my constant drive to upgrade my skills was, in reality, a perverse reaction to a deeply embedded sense of inadequacy. I had always believed that when I approached or reached professional competence, I would overcome this ever-present lack of self-confidence that made it so difficult to accept new challenges and move into leadership positions.

So, despite reaching my present relatively high level of training, my habitual anxiety and tension with its associated state of discontent, my constant fear of failing, my lack of assertiveness and indecision remained barriers toward advancement. No longer could these entrenched personality and emotional weaknesses be clothed with the excuse of a disadvantaged educational or social position. I know now that the employment crisis I was then facing was caused by emotional and psychological factors I could not address intellectually.

Although technically qualified, I was unable to compete successfully for a newly opened supervisor's position in our department. This was a personal failure despite my senior status. The person finally chosen was much better qualified in terms of leadership and supervisory abilities. He had proven administration experience and met the requirements of the position completely. My technical qualifications, even if superior, and this itself was questionable, would have been a small part of that position in any case.

To make matters worse, the weaknesses that kept me from that promotion also kept me from understanding I would not have succeeded in that role (I recall the current, if cynical, corporate shibboleth: "People rise to the level of their incompetence"). Ideally, had I the spiritual insight then that makes this whole situation clear to me now, I would have recognized the validity of the choice management made, and graciously accepted the supporting role in which I could have been successful and happy. Lacking that insight and because of imagined affronts to my dignity and pride, I decided to look for another job.

But spiritual ignorance does not provide spiritual insight, and it was the ego-driven sins of immature anger, envy and false pride that motivated my actions and feelings, resulting in this irrational and potentially destructive decision. Although I talked of better opportunities, more money, and a shorter commute to work as my reasons for quitting, I knew it was out of those baser motives that moved me to look for a another place to work and the economic climate of the day made it possible for me to find one in short order.

Despite the poor basis for that decision, I rapidly carved out a productive niche for myself in the Research and Development department of my new company. I continued to study and upgrade my skills, and in measured steps I moved from technician, to senior technician, to engineering aide. It was here that a latent talent I had for writing technical information was discovered. At one point, I was "loaned" to the Publications Department to help write the instruction manual for equipment with which I worked closely in its developmental stages. I moved into that department on a permanent basis as a technical writer, and in time I was able to overcome my lack of professional credentials: that is, formal accredited schooling, that kept me an hourly paid employee. Finally, when I was accorded professional status and placed in a salaried and supervisory position, I felt I had accomplished a major life goal.

By the middle of the 1960s, the two main areas of my life, work and family, appeared as mirror images in terms of satisfaction and fulfillment. Our seventh child was born and our first was now four-teen. Our small house was crowded, and today it seems incredible we were all accommodated, but with judicious partitioning we somehow managed. Our children's perspective of those years will be different, I am sure, from those of their parents, however, for us these were productive and fulfilling years. The physical environment was ideal for their upbringing. It was well-forested with many nearby fields, gardens and some farms. We enjoyed a nearby community lake, no further than a few minutes walk for swimming and boating in the summer and ice skating and seasonal sports in the winter. And within these large areas of open space, the neighborhood was teeming with all age groups.

To complete this utopian picture, the town was secure and protected with a traditional New England atmosphere. Nevertheless, it was close enough to New York City to be in its cultural and intellectual orbit. Children growing up here thus enjoyed a somewhat mixed lifestyle: the benefits of a rural setting and proximity to a major metropolitan center. And the schools completed what could only be described as a parent's dream.

As I write these words, now many years later, I look out my window and realize I am looking at the same environment, little changed but with a new generation of parents and children poised to accept its gifts. I reflect on that time, when Florence and I made that fateful decision to buy this lot, little knowing the enormous consequences of that inspired judgment. If only for that reason alone, I marvel at the extraordinary, often bizarre, always impenetrable twists and turns of an ordinary life. No justification needs be summoned for the acknowledgment of a divine blessing. If I expressed these thoughts to many neighbors who over the years came and left this same area, they would say I was dreaming. And they would be right. But no matter; what is or is not a dream, after all, has less to do with the dream than with the dreamer.

Just as I came to believe this new and joyful convergence of my family and employment lives was on a solid foundation, an odd juxtaposition in my life developed. As my work situation became more stable, productive, and satisfying (in a word, ideal), these idyllic family circumstances were challenged by the chaotic forces of normal adolescence and abnormal social disorder. This was the late '60s; we had four teens in the house, and our oldest daughter was preparing for college. As the old familiar employment-related anxieties were diminishing, and they certainly were no longer overshadowing, new stresses emerged at home due to the chaotic social turbulence particularly affecting high school and college age students.

Widespread drug and alcohol use, college rioting and early sex fueled the ever-present fear, especially on my part as I remembered my own adolescence, that youthful errors could distort and threaten their promising futures. Both Florence and I lived fairly abstemious, health-conscious lives. I knew, however, from my own history the limits of parental influence on youthful willfulness. My fears for my children's well-being were a constant presence, loosened only by the onset of my spiritual practice to come some six years later.

It did not take quite as long to fall off the mountain top as it did to climb it. In 1970, two years after I reached professional status, the nation's priorities changed and my space-program-based company was forced into a bankruptcy reorganization and I lost my job.

My financial situation was not critical as Florence was by then working part-time. Our mortgage was a small one and almost paid off. As my children reached college age this status made them less a strain on our resources than their staying at home would have been, because their education was largely self-financed. Ironically, one of the consequences of my inability to earn a large salary and to acquire commensurate financial resources was to provide them eligibility for student loans, grants, scholarships and work-study programs. Consequently, six of them were able to put themselves through college, with several acquiring advanced degrees.

Despite this relatively good personal position, a completely unanticipated, and irrational, panic set in, making a realistic evaluation of my situation impossible. After a few futile weeks of trying to get a position reflecting my skill level, I began to think I was not really qualified, after all, for work on a professional level. I was faced once again with the question of credentials and education and prospective employers were not, especially in this market, interested in past performance as sole justification for hiring me.

I lost my confidence and lowered my sights, eventually taking an entry level job in a dead-end position. The next five years were in many ways a repetition and a summary of the employment experience of my earlier life. I was doing work I did not like and struggled to perform properly. The former anxieties and crises of self-confidence reemerged although moderated and weakened by the previous years of achievement. Also, for the first time, I began to question my parenting, as my children were forging ahead with plans that often conflicted with what we would have thought best for them. I began then to look at my state of life as the continuation of a long pattern of conflicted behavior and temperament stretching into an unhappy and bitter future.

Against this, however, there were important new factors. My previous successes left their mark on me and moderated my sense of failure. I believed that what I was able to do once I would be able to do again, but this was an intellectual exercise. I could not know then that anxiety, fear, feelings of inadequacy, all such negativity, are born in the ignorance of a hidden spiritual center, their dissolution awaiting only the opening of the door to the soul. Knowing well these pernicious feelings and understanding them to be weakness to be overcome can do little more than to bring them to a conscious level. But bringing these sentiments to this level has its value later when their dissolution reveals the power of spiritual practice.

It was then, during that general period of soul searching and assessment, in another example of the perfect timing that marked my life, that my son brought home Maharishi's timeless message promising new frontiers. I was ready. My preparatory years were complete; one lifetime ended; a new lifetime was to begin.

Foundations

*T*he knowledge that life can be lived without anxiety and fear had become concrete in my consciousness even within the relatively short time after my initiation into Transcendental Meditation. The return of negative emotions, although disappointing, could not dispel the effects of reaching this new level of consciousness. These anxious episodes remained uncomfortable and unwelcome, but no matter how intense they were, there was never a complete over-shadowing; there was always a sense of the Absolute. Indeed, at times the episodes themselves were a reminder of the Absolute.

This new sense of a transcendent presence in my life created a strong urge for understanding. The scientific explanations of my experiences as physiological or psychological events had, as I indicated, little significance for me. They were strangely unsatisfying. From the second lecture introducing TM, I had learned that this meditation was brought to the West by an Indian monk from the ancient Vedic tradition of India. But it was suggested that these origins were secondary. Meditation has value for the West because of the universality of the technique in human terms, not because there was intrinsic value in Eastern thought.

Much like the application of the law of gravity discovered by the English scientist, Isaac Newton, the law worked as well in India as it did in England, of course, but can one ignore the science and philosophy on which it is based? Obviously, to do so would cut oneself off from the underlying knowledge that supported it, in this case, the culture of Western Enlightenment. For this reason, as my practice continued, I started to search out, understand, and appreciate the ancient tradition underlying this system of meditation.

I began to realize why the teaching of meditation was developed in these terms; if a broad section of a modern, i.e. Western, population were to accept this program it would have to be taught in their language, with their vocabulary. Indeed, when speaking to others about meditation, I used the very same language I found unsatisfactory for myself because I did not have the spiritual understanding, confidence, or the vernacular to talk about it differently. Later, after some immersion in the Eastern and Western mystical tradition, I learned to appreciate Maharishi's accomplishment in recasting the language of the Vedic tradition to make it available to the West.

Then, however, for reasons I would not begin to understand for a long time, there was something much more important unfolding than these explanations suggested. I know now I was swept into a river of understanding that has its source in a time beyond memory, but which waters every generation in human communities all over the world, and which bubbles up today in tiny Third-World villages as well as giant First-World cities. Nothing less than this cosmic connection, in my mind, would have done justice to what I felt.

In "New Age" language, I entered the flow where life is lived without effort and strain. In the Vedic tradition of India, where this awareness has always been part of the culture and expressly cultivated, celebrated in song and story, this state of consciousness is called *turiya,* or the "fourth" state. The Mandukya Upanishad, a classic exposition of this aspect of Vedic philosophy, lists four conditions of life: deep, dreamless sleep; the dreaming state; the waking or conscious state; and the fourth state:

> The Fourth, say the wise, is not subjective experience,
> nor objective experience, nor experience intermediate
> between these two, nor is it a negative condition which
> is neither consciousness nor unconsciousness. It is not
> the knowledge of the senses, nor is it relative knowledge,
> nor yet inferential knowledge. Beyond the senses,
> beyond the understanding, beyond all expression, is the
> Fourth. It is pure unitary consciousness, wherein aware-
> ness of the world and of multiplicity is completely
> obliterated. It is ineffable peace. It is the supreme good.
> It is One without a second. It is the Self. Know it alone.[1]

This description of the fourth state of consciousness is the
Vedic explanation of transcendental consciousness, and it is the
foundation, in fact, of my new mode of functioning and understanding.

The time arrived when more and more exposure to this new
state of awareness, coupled with increased knowledge, allowed me
the additional joy to establish this practice in its universal context.
I came to understand, I thought, C. G. Jung's concept of the
"collective unconscious," the idea of deep levels of the unconscious
mind connecting humankind. I amended that concept, however,
by discarding the notion of an "unconscious" and accepting the
Vedic idea of a continuum of consciousness allowing the individual
conscious awareness of these deep levels of human association.

This universality that I had been sensing experientially began
to take a more substantial form when I discovered descriptions of
this transcendent state in the literature of all major religious and
spiritual traditions. In his classic book, *Mysticism and Philosophy*,
W.T. Stace explores the phenomenon of the universality of this
state of consciousness. After quoting the Upanishadic description
of turiya, Stace redefines it in more familiar Western terms:

> ...mystics—thousands of them all over the world—unan-
> imously assert that they have attained to this complete

vacuum of particular mental contents, but that what then happens is quite different from a lapse in[to] unconsciousness. On the contrary, what emerges is a state of *pure* consciousness—"pure" in the sense that it is not the consciousness of any empirical content. It has no content except itself.[2]

Religious, spiritual and philosophical literature are replete with illustrations that depict that state of consciousness described above. But they had become accessible to me only now. When St. Teresa of Avila, guiding her sisters through the confusion of spiritual growth, wrote: "Oh, what a great blessing is this state in which that accursed one can do us no harm! Great are the gains which come to the soul with God working in it and neither we ourselves nor anyone else hindering Him."[3] I found those words resonating in my being and I felt guided and inspired by them.

The Upanishadic teaching of ancient times, its echo in modern philosophical literature, and its reverberation in classic mystical spiritualism were only a hint of the extent of the spiritual life beginning to infuse my consciousness. These variations in time and place only enhanced the sense of their universality. But, more importantly, the realization emerged that this teaching is as relevant and as vital to the life of modern man as it was to the ordinary people of past ages. The great modern tragedy, indeed, is that this knowledge, though never completely lost, has been overshadowed and relegated to abstruse intellectual dust bins by the powerful and productive ideas of scientific enlightenment. In his book, *Modern Man in Search of a Soul*, C.G. Jung describes this "completely modern" man as one who has left behind and discarded his past and traditions, and has become "'unhistorical' in the deepest sense."[4] "The modern man," Jung would say, "has lost all the metaphysical certainties of his medieval brother, and set up in their place the ideals of material security, general welfare and humaneness."[5]

Only in recent decades has the notion emerged, perhaps resurfaced is better put, that people living active family, social and economic lives have identical spiritual lives to those austere and reclusive mystics. And though the tumult of modern life distorts and hides it, this spirituality is similarly subject to discovery and growth. Moreover, like their reclusive counterparts, this spiritual life transforms and fulfills them. It is not surprising, therefore, to find those experiencing this "new" spirituality identifying with and reclaiming its traditional history, thereby escaping from what Jung lamented as modern man's "unhistorical" status. The expressions "state of enlightenment" and "cosmic consciousness" are no longer confined to esoteric practices or remote ashrams and monasteries.

The Indian, Chinese, Arabic (Islam), Judaic, and Eastern Orthodox traditions have recognized the state of enlightenment historically as an integral part of and, indeed, the purpose of their spiritual practices. In European Christianity this level of consciousness was never part of its mainstream theology. From its inception, the Roman Church has recognized the existence of people, Christians and others, experiencing this state of consciousness, but this recognition often meant condemnation rather than approval as indicated by Church destruction of early Christian Gnostics. Nevertheless, it did shelter, despite its ambivalence and the work of the "Holy" Inquisition, a two-thousand-year tradition of contemplatives whose lives clearly indicate the deep roots of this experience in universal consciousness.

It is from the Vedas, however, that the most ancient, clearest, and consistent description of this state comes down to us: what it is, how it is recognized, how it is acquired and the nature of the way it is experienced. In an ancient Indian tradition, Vedic wisdom is revealed knowledge, cognized through spiritual practices millennia ago and passed down through various oral traditions at first, then through written literature as a later development. The guru and chela (or teacher and pupil) relationship is integral to that tradition.

The *Bhagavad Gita* is the central jewel in the crown of this literature. It was translated into English by Charles Wilkins in 1785, the first translation of a Sanskrit document into English. It was then translated into German and Latin by Friedrich and August von Schlegel who were introduced to Sanskrit by Alexander Hamilton. Hamilton was returning from India in 1802 and was required to remain in Paris because of the war.[6] This discovery of Sanskrit led to the comparative study of languages and modern linguistics, and it also introduced the Vedic concept of the Absolute, or Brahman, into Europe and America.

But it remained for living representatives of this tradition, Indian Masters, who first made their way to the West starting in the last years of the 19th century, to establish this teaching as an integral component of Western consciousness. Continuing well into the second half of the 20th century, they succeeded in firmly planting this knowledge and, more importantly, the methods for its acquisition. This introduction of Vedic teaching could be said to have reached the West in three distinct waves: the Vedanta societies organized by Swami Vivekananda to spread the teaching of the 19th century Indian saint, Ramakrishna; the Self-Realization Fellowship of Paramahansa Yogananda; and the Transcendental Meditation (TM) movement of Maharishi Mahesh Yogi.

Swami Vivekananda, charged by Ramakrishna at his death in 1886 to spread his teachings, first went to Europe and then to the United States to establish Ramakrishna Missions. In his book, *My Guru and His Disciple*, Christopher Isherwood describes the nature of these missions and his own very personal relationship with his guru, Swami Prabhavananda, from 1939, the date of his initiation into Vedanta, until Prabhavananda's death in 1976. He remained a disciple until his own death in 1986. These missions founded at the turn of the century during Vivekananda's last visit to the United States "were often called Vedanta societies, meaning that they were dedicated to the study and practice of the philosophy which is taught in the Vedas, the most ancient of the Hindu scriptures."[7]

The Vedanta societies were heavily influenced by Indian ritual, religious language and the traditional guru/chela relationships. This made it difficult, if not impossible, for the basic core of Vedic wisdom to find its way out of narrow intellectual and philosophical circles to a broader Western population. Even Isherwood, devoted to Prabhavananda as he was (he considered at one time entering the monastic life with him), would often feel, "the Swami is too Indian for me." After Prabhavananda's death, Isherwood gave voice to this characteristic of the Ramakrishna missions:

> His physical absence doesn't make nearly as much difference to me as I had expected it would. I think about him as constantly as I ever did. What I do seem to be losing touch with is Swami's Hindu pantheon of gods, goddesses, and divine incarnations. My Occidental consciousness is in the process of rejecting them, it seems as imperfectly transplanted culturally foreign bodies.[8]

Vedanta societies continue to function in the West inspiring those individuals whose souls find sustenance in the teaching and life of Ramakrishna.

Paramahansa Yogananda, the leader of the "second wave," was born in India in 1893. His life's story, *Autobiography of a Yogi*, is an enduring classic of Vedic spirituality and defines another period in the introduction of Vedic wisdom into Western consciousness. Yogananda's father worked in a professional capacity for the Bengal-Nagpur Railway and the family apparently enjoyed the economic status equivalent to the Western upper middle-class.

Although "living in the world," both parents were disciples of Lahiri Mahasaya, a Yogic Master in a tradition of Masters that unites Krishna and Jesus Christ, East and West, and their household was suffused by these influences. Yogananda's early impulses toward the spiritual life were therefore greatly encouraged, especially by his mother. In 1914, his lifelong desire became a reality when his guru, Sri Yukteswar, initiated him as a monk in the Swami Giri Order.[9]

Like Swami Vivekananda before him, Yogananda was destined to travel to the United States to bring the Vedic teachings of his Master to the West. Indeed, when Sri Yukteswar performed the traditional Swami induction ceremony he used dyed silk as the symbol of the renunciant's robe: "Someday you will go to the West, where silk is preferred," he said. "As a symbol, I have chosen for you this silk material instead of the customary cotton."[10] In 1917, Yogananda inaugurated the Yogoda Satsanga Society (Self-Realization Fellowship), which was dedicated to the teachings of the tradition of Masters represented by Sri Yukteswar and Lahiri Mahasaya, which is known as *kriya yoga*. Shortly after having a vision where he saw himself in America, Yogananda was invited to represent India, in Boston in 1920, at an International Congress of Religious Liberals under the auspices of the American Unitarian Association.[11] In her introduction to a collection of Yogananda's lectures, *Man's Eternal Quest*, one of his American successors, Sri Daya Mata, provides a snapshot of this visit:

> For more than a decade he traveled the length and breadth of America, speaking almost daily to capacity audiences in all the major cities. On January 28, 1925, the "Los Angeles Times" reported: "The Philharmonic Auditorium presents the extraordinary spectacle of thousands...being turned away an hour before the advertised opening of a lecture with the 3000-seat hall filled to its utmost capacity. Swami Yogananda is the attrac-

tion. A Hindu invading the United States to bring God...preaching the essence of Christian doctrine." It came as no small revelation to the West that Yoga—so eloquently expounded and clearly interpreted by Sri Yogananda—is a universal science, and that as such it is indeed the "essence" of all true religions.[12]

In 1925, in Los Angeles, Yogananda founded the Self-Realization Fellowship's international headquarters and began the next stage of his mission, the founding of Self-Realization Fellowship temples and centers, "To reveal the complete harmony and basic oneness of original Christianity as taught by Jesus Christ and original Yoga as taught by Bhagavan Krishna; and to show that these principles of truth are the common scientific foundation of all true religions," as one section of its *Aims and Ideals* states.[13] For the past seventy years this knowledge has found a secure place in Western consciousness through the continued activity of Yogananda's Self-Realization Fellowship.

When another Indian Master, Maharishi Mahesh Yogi, established the first center of his Spiritual Regeneration Movement (SRM) in San Francisco on March 30, 1959, sixty years after Vivekananda's Vedanta societies and thirty-five years after Yogananda's SRF temples, it signaled the arrival of a new wave of that teaching, a new wave of that Vedic ocean. This was not a new message, Maharishi would say, "this is the same old message of Krishna, the same message of Christ" (that the Kingdom of God is within you). But what was new, or rather, "rediscovered," was a simple, ancient technique, called Transcendental Meditation (TM), that allowed any person of any profession or religion, of any social status—a reclusive monk or worldly citizen—to enter into that state of consciousness, samadhi or bliss, which is the goal of the Vedic teachings. Maharishi's message was simple and to the point for all people, "if you can think, you can meditate." In a 1960 lecture, in Cambridge, England, on "Deep Meditation" Maharishi said:

The word, "meditation," is not new. The gains from meditation are not new to be counted. But the information that it is easy for everyone to meditate and experience the inner glories of life—this seems to be a new message.

Although the message is centuries, centuries old message. [sic] The same age-old message of Buddha, the same age-old message of Christ, the same age-old message of Krishna; get within, experience the Kingdom of Heaven; experience Nirvana; experience eternal freedom; come out with that freedom, live a life of freedom in the world. The same age-old message.[14]

Unlike his spiritual and national compatriots, Maharishi, at first, never felt a special need or impulse to bring the teachings of his Master, Swami Brahmananda Saraswati, (called Guru Dev by Maharishi and meditators worldwide) to a general world population. He met Swami Brahmananda while still an undergraduate physics student and was instructed to finish his studies. Three years later, in 1940, Swami Brahmananda was induced to leave his reclusive life and become Shankaracharya of Joytir Math, the north Indian monastery founded by Shankara. Maharishi joined him there and for the next thirteen years was content to live in his shadow; "The whole purpose was just to attune myself with Guru Dev, and that was all that I wanted to do."[15]

With Guru Dev's passing in 1953, Maharishi journeyed to the Himalayas intent on living a reclusive life. He entered into the caves of the "Valley of the Saints" in Uttar Kashi. In an account of this time, he describes a period about two years after he arrived when he began to sense the notion of Rameshvaram, a town in the southern part of India. The thought persisted for several months and presented a problem, "what to do with this thought?"

I quite remember, there was absolutely no purpose attached to this thought of Rameshvaram. I didn't know myself why the thought was coming up. Absolutely nothing. Rameshvaram. I didn't know what I'd do when I went there and what I was going there for.[16]

Finally, to deal with this impulse once and for all he decided to visit Rameshvaram with the intention of returning when his mission, whatever it was, was finished. Subsequently, he spent several weeks in southern India visiting temples and shrines until he sensed the time for his return to the north. The contrast between his fifteen years or more in the bliss of the Himalayas and the terrible suffering experienced by India's masses revealed in all its terrible clarity "the two realities: life being lived on a completely wretched level and life described on the most exalted level."[17]

Before returning, he felt he should give the blessings of the Himalayas to the people, but what form those blessings should take he did not know; only "...that something should be done so that people don't suffer, because there is no reason to suffer...."[18] How that decision was to be implemented, however, was taken out of his hands. Stopping off in the city of Trivandrum, the capital of Kerala, on his way back to Uttar Kashi, Maharishi was asked to speak at the local library. This was not only completely unexpected, but also lecturing was something he had never done.

Nevertheless, he found himself scheduled to speak for the next seven days. His message to the townspeople of Trivandrum was simple enough, the blessings of the Himalayas were available to the householder no less than to the holy mendicant. The blissful nature of transcendence can be incorporated into the daily life of all people. For the first time in many centuries this long forgotten theme now revived by Maharishi's master was spoken out to the masses:

Everywhere Maharishi's message was the same—the suffering and misery so common to human existence are unnecessary. Life in its essential nature is bliss, and every person can experience unbounded bliss consciousness and integrate it into daily life through the effortless technique of Transcendental Meditation.[19]

The identity of the man who tapped Maharishi on the shoulder on a dusty temple road in Trivandrum has been lost forever, but that one seemingly innocent action fixed Maharish's future and changed the lives of millions the world over. The reception to his lectures and to the system of meditation he taught was so over-whelming that an organization and following soon emerged, and Maharishi found himself traveling from town to town speaking and teaching.

For the next two years Maharishi traveled the rest of India bringing this teaching to tens of thousands of people. At the end of 1957 Maharishi was asked how he would like to celebrate the anniversary of Guru Dev's 89th birthday. It was decided to organize a Seminar of Spiritual Luminaries in Madras on the last three days of December to bring together Swami Brahmananda's disciples, saints from all over India, and thousands of ordinary people. In a talk at this Seminar, Maharishi reviewed the preceding two years' successes in teaching Transcendental Meditation, its simplicity and its effects, and asked spontaneously, "Why can't we spiritually regenerate the whole world through this technique?"[20] Thus, on January 1st, 1958 the Spiritual Regeneration Movement was born, eventually to find its way to San Francisco on that special March day in 1959.

The following principles are common to all spiritual traditions that have Vedic scripture or literature as their source: there is a transcendental level of existence, a nonsensory field, unbounded, without attributes, the Absolute; this field upholds and sustains the material world and it is accessible to the human nervous system. Furthermore, the purpose of life is to achieve awareness of this field and union with it as a condition of personal existence, and this union, or yoga, translates as a state of enlightenment. But it is the approach to this union that makes the teachings of Swami Brahmananda unique. As Maharishi never tires of describing: its main feature is a simple technique, available to any thinking man, without years of preparation, and easily incorporated into modern life and can be learned in a matter of hours. This program is the practical foundation for the entirety of Vedic knowledge.

Unique as this approach to Vedic teaching is, Maharishi was uniquely qualified to interpret it. His training as a physicist allowed him to recast the often obscure, esoteric and mystical language of ancient metaphysical texts into ideas accessible to the modern scientific mind. With the availability of growing numbers of meditators, controlled scientific experiments on the physiological and psychological effects of meditation could be undertaken. In 1970, Robert Keith Wallace earned his doctorate in physiology at the University of California, Los Angeles, proposing and demonstrating the ancient Vedic state of consciousness, turiya. Wallace discovered and documented the physiological correlates of a fourth major state of consciousness, as described in the Upanishads, in people practicing the Transcendental Meditation technique. This venerable component of human wisdom, so long known in the East, glimpsed by scholars and philosophers of the West in only the past two centuries, had finally entered and become integrated into the consciousness of Western man.

Since that time hundreds of studies in universities throughout the world have replicated and validated the physiological effects of meditation. There is general agreement that the quantifiable response of the meditative state tends to move the physiology in the direction of optimum health. Shortly after Wallace's breakthrough findings at UCLA, Harvard researchers successfully repeated and extended the research using the large pool of meditating students in the Cambridge area with the cooperation of Maharishi's Students International Meditating Society.[21] But none of these scientific studies, important and necessary as they may have been, provided the link connecting modern "yogis," "mystics," and "saints" to their spiritual ancestors.

What did make this connection, however, and what could only have made this connection, was the subjective experience of this "fourth" state as reported by thousands of people—well-known or obscure, attached or unattached to a particular religion or ideology, whose experiential descriptions affirm this bond of understanding and identity. Thus, when a modern meditator reports:

> I experience a state of complete silence devoid of any motion, a state of unboundedness and total ease in deep relaxation. There are no thoughts, no feelings or any other sensations like weight or temperature. I just know 'I am.' There is no notion of time and space but my mind is fully aware and perfectly clear. It is a very natural and simple state.[22]

the person echoes the ancient seer of the Mandukya Upanishad quoted earlier, "Beyond the senses, beyond the understanding, beyond all expression, is the Fourth." This transcendental state of consciousness, the goal and promise of my new practice, I now understood to be the foundation of living a life in freedom through spiritual transformation.

CHAPTER SIX

The Teachers I

The saying, "when the student is ready the teacher will come," has reached the level of cliche. But its apparent triteness hides deep ancient truths that are revealed as students uncover new dimensions of consciousness in themselves. A spontaneous redefinition of the concept of "teacher" is one expression of this. Traditionally, the teacher is one who instructs and guides, leads and pushes, exhorts and threatens, but is generally thought of as another person. By expanding this definition, however, the spiritual seeker finds in life's activities—such as a book suddenly acquired, an event or a person strangely met, perhaps a flash of intuition often in the onset of a crisis—an illumination of such magnitude that questions and answers emerge simultaneously in the mind. This interior emergence is as representative of the coming of the teacher as the physical meeting of a guru, although recognition of the former may be subtle and long after the fact.

Paramahansa Yogananda's *Autobiography of a Yogi* had been lying around the house for a while, the discarded remnant of someone's college course. That word "Yogi" in the title and also in Maharishi's name was its only connection for me. As I started to read it, I recognized immediately what it was that tied Maharishi and Yogananda together: they both taught the reality of the transcendent and its accessibility. Beyond that, however, they seemed to have little else in common.

While the TM centers, under Maharishi's guidance, explained

the benefits of experiencing transcendence in the unsatisfying terms, (at least for me) of "the psychobiology of consciousness," Yogananda wrote of the unfolding of spiritual development in terms which demanded the denial of, or at least, the suspension of a normal, modern, common sense understanding of the world— something I found very difficult to do. I could not give credence to the reports he described of the feats and abilities of his saints and yogis. My problem was a simple one: Maharishi's explanations were not "spiritual" enough, and Yogananda's were not rational enough.

Nevertheless, I recognized in Yogananda's book that my meditation was tied to age-old traditions that inspired me and gave rise to a desire to connect with them. Yogananda provided intuitive insights of Maharishi's practice, which somehow drew me closer to my own meditation. Out of the disparity of these two commentaries on my new spiritual life, neither of which was wholly acceptable, was the first realization that this meditation was apart from any specific teaching; it was a spiritual river that became stronger and greater as diverse streams of knowledge, made up of major sources and tiny rivulets, entered and merged with it.

The year after initiation, the beginning of an indefinite period, was lived on two levels. I fulfilled all my family and work responsibilities, diligently I thought, but at the same time I found myself consciously observing new personal modes of functioning and thinking. I spent as many weekends as I could at meditation residence courses and at the TM center, snapping like a hungry fish at any morsel of information offering an explanation of these continuing life changes. That these activities caused less strain in my domestic situation than they could have, was less due to me than to my wife and children. Florence was tolerant and supportive, if confused, and the children were all of an age when their interests were almost completely self-centered. At work, however, new ideas were starting to ferment as I prepared, or more properly, as I was being prepared, to encounter new worlds of understanding.

My work was becoming less interesting and less fulfilling as a new confidence developed and I sensed the restoration of a lost faith in myself that I had not felt for a long time. I say "restoration" deliberately. I had described the loss I felt when the first professional position I achieved was snatched from under me, and then out of panic and depression I moved once again to a dead-end job.

Now, some seven years later, after a slow and difficult climb through several job changes to some semblance of my former professional status, my new spiritual experiences produced an upsurge of renewed confidence and self-worth. I decided to reenter the job market on this new level. I updated my resume to emphasize my technical writing experience and submitted it to an employment agency, more to test the waters than in expectation that these initial offerings would bear fruit. I was absolutely amazed when I received a call two days later that I should arrange time for a preliminary interview. Within ten days I had a new job as a Technical Writer, albeit in a junior capacity, in a salaried position rather than as an hourly worker, and the prospects of a new career unfolded before me.

When the "head hunter" handling my case told me that he had worked with this company for several years and this was the first time they ever turned an application around for him within two weeks, my growing spiritual awareness made it easy for me to embrace the idea of a "guiding spirit" supporting my efforts. I was not looking for a sign of revealed wisdom, but the situation was, I thought, a perfect example of "the support of nature." This was a newly learned Vedic concept that says that meditation brings one's life into accord with the laws of nature, where one's intentions become spontaneously life-supporting and rapidly fulfilled. If this was, indeed, an example of the preternatural support meditators obtain, it was also, as we will see, an example of the surreal twists and turns this support can take as people move to the places they have to be and find the teachers they need to meet.

If the experience in getting my new job was any indication of the support of nature, all that great natural law support I received in obtaining my new position presumably would continue, leading me to fulfillment in realizing the career goals it thus opened. In fact, the complete opposite took place. Within three months I was informed that my work was less than satisfactory, and three months later I was terminated. The fact that my supervisor accepted responsibility for "misjudging" my level of ability, and assured me of supportive references to a prospective new employer, could not lessen the reality of my situation, which was identical to the traumatic one seven years earlier.

But this was only one side of that six-month period; as disastrous as it seemed on the surface, it had an equally extraordinary impact on my hidden spiritual development.

Shortly after I had started this new job, Robert B., another new employee, became my office mate. Robert was a professional in every way I was not. He had a degree in Engineering. He had taught English and music and played in a local orchestra. But most important for me, he organized and led a local Theosophical Society group. He and his wife Janice became my guides into an entirely new world of esoteric and New Age knowledge.

Modern Theosophy is a revival of an ancient teaching institutionalized in the Theosophical Society (TS), founded in the United States in 1875 by Madame Helena Petrovna Blavatsky and Colonel H. S. Olcott. The purpose of the TS was to disseminate the hidden doctrines and natural mysteries discovered, studied and sheltered by an unique school of Tibetan Buddhist Masters with whom Madame Blavatsky was in personal and psychic contact.

These esoteric teachings, described in her book, *The Secret Doctrine*, were made available in the West as new knowledge, and in the East, especially India, where the once-lost knowledge was to be revived.

I started to attend a small Theosophical discussion circle in early 1978 led by Robert. The roots of modern Theosophy sink deeply into that exotic world of Madame Blavatsky and her spiritual and physical contacts with highly evolved Masters and Adepts. Despite changes over the years, the basic Theosophical principles remain. These involve ideas of karma, reincarnation, the goals of life, the nature of the subtle worlds between death and rebirth, and, not the last or the least, the Masters or Mahatmas existing in a Hierarchy who guide and develop individuals and groups for personal and universal spiritual growth. I was exhilarated, satisfied, and excited by these ideas, and in some way comforted.

I felt a kinship with these teachings because they dealt with levels of consciousness I was becoming increasingly familiar with; areas discernible in both my meditative practice and normal waking state consciousness. There was no question of evaluating the "truth" of these ideas. I did not worry that they were or were not consistent with what I learned elsewhere, mainly as part of my TM program. Actually, I did not think in terms of this being "right" or that being "wrong." What I began to realize then, a realization that was to continuously deepen, was that all evaluations were limited to a rational and scientific understanding of the world. These words and this knowledge, however, addressed another aspect of my psyche; an aspect of my being that responded emotionally, without thoughts, but with feelings of joy, comfort, agreement, and a sense of up-welling bliss. I experienced all these visceral impulses in meditation, and, as when in activity, they directed my attention inward. In a way, they became another positive and valuable part of my meditative life.

For several months I met with the TS group, finding many areas of common interest and understanding that continue to be a part of an integrated understanding of the world. However, when it became obvious that remaining part of this group would require a deeper commitment than I was willing to make, especially in terms of meditative practice, I obeyed a growing desire to stop meeting with them. This may have been more of a problem for me than for the TS society, which made no personal demands, but I resisted any activity that threatened to modify or supplant my TM practice. Over the years, this instinctual recognition developed into a faithful principle, one I held to and encourage others to hold to: enjoy the fullness of the heavenly orchestra, but stay with and become the master of your own instrument.

Because my contacts with Robert and Janice were ongoing, this new dimension of knowledge continued to expand as I dove deeper into the ocean of New Age philosophy. Janice managed the local book store which had a large selection of New Age and occult material. Beside Theosophical material, I found a seemingly inexhaustible range of literature on paranormal knowledge. A truly new psychological parameter opened, permitting exploration of unknown worlds following the footsteps of the most diverse psychic explorers imaginable. Once out of the structural limitations imposed by the requirements of rationality and logic, the world takes on a miraculous quality in which anything is possible and any idea can be valid. Some of these explorations were and remain peripheral to my experience, but others became central and integrated into a new worldview.

Thus I became acquainted with the insights and observations of personalities like Seth, a "person" who visited the writer, Jane Roberts, for many years from places and times we cannot fathom.

Seth, through Roberts' mediumship, provided purportedly experiential insights into reincarnation, karma, life after death, health and the nature of physical reality. I found myself integrating the knowledge Seth was transmitting through Roberts into a growing perspective that was able to accommodate the orthodox Vedic teachings undergirding my TM practice. The ideas of "finding reality within us," or of "spontaneous knowing," I found familiar and representative of my experience. I understood Roberts perfectly when she wrote about the difficulty of revelatory knowledge: "The trouble is that we must somehow translate the data into terms that we can understand, explaining it verbally or with images—and distortions are bound to result. Some experiences can't be expressed physically, yet the individual concerned is convinced of their validity."[1]

Examples of America's classical spiritual, spiritualist, and psychic heritage came into my awareness and possession. One such was Levi's *The Aquarian Gospel of Jesus the Christ,* the product of an American 19th-century mystic's visionary readings from the Akashic Records. These "records," it is explained, are the indelible impressions of a "Universal Mind" which yields universal knowledge to one attuned to it. The "Gospel" is a revealed record of the life of Jesus from birth through his teaching mission and final achievement, including the "lost" eighteen years of his life.

The concept of the Aquarian Age comes from our familiar Zodiac, which represents the orbit of our solar system around a distant fixed point—fixed, of course, only relative to our sun. It takes almost 26,000 years for a complete orbit, so each sign of the Zodiac requires a little more than 2,100 years for the sun's transit. Jesus lived early in the sign of the fish, Pisces, when his earthly life commenced. We are now at the end of the Piscean Age and entering the Age of Aquarius, which, the "Aquarian Gospel" tells us, will fulfill the vision and teachings of Jesus the Christ.

Levi records the Holy family's escape to Egypt when Jesus was an infant, the early recognition by Hebrew and Indian sages of his special qualities and his education in the hidden mysteries of the Hebrew and Vedic spiritual traditions. In those years, so strangely missing from orthodox text, Levi reveals Jesus' life and work in India, Tibet, Persia, Assyria, Greece and Egypt before commencing his culminating work as the Christ, or Messiah. For reasons I could not then, or even now, explain, I was inspired and moved by this narration.

In this context I should mention another American mystic, Edgar Cayce, whose life and work spanned the latter part of the 19th-century to almost the middle of the 20th. Cayce interacted and influenced the spiritual and physical lives of many thousands of people during his lifetime and his teachings continue to do so even today. He was born in Kentucky, in March 1877 into a traditional American farming family. His grandfather, Thomas Jefferson Cayce, possessed unusual mystical gifts, including the ability to find water, or dowsing, and psychokinesis. The grandparents and grandson were very close but tied together by more than kinship. Young Cayce inherited his grandfather's psychic abilities. But, where these abilities seemed only an adjunct to the life of his grandfather, they were destined to determine the fate of Edgar's. In those early years he began to exhibit certain paranormal abilities, which included spiritual visits and conversations with his now dead grandfather, reported only to his grandmother who saw her husband's gifts replicated in Edgar. He also discovered an ability to "read" his school books simply by "sleeping a little on them" and then upon awakening he knew their contents.

Although he continued to experience extraordinary events in his adolescence, they started to fade as he matured and sought a more urban occupation outside the Cayce farm tradition. His life as a psychic began in March 1901 by accident; when as a last desperate attempt to treat his own serious throat ailment, he found he could diagnose and cure it while in a hypnotic trance. It was then discovered that when in a trance he could diagnose and provide treatment for others, remarkably, needing only their name or an other minimally identifying factor.

For more than twenty years following that strange beginning, he made thousands of medical conditions, or physical, "readings." In 1923, in response to a first-time request to make other than a physical reading, he tried to cast an astrological chart for one Arthur Lammers, when, "almost at the end of the reading, and still in staccato, noncommittal style, came the curious sentence: 'He was once a monk.'"[2] From that first suggestion of reincarnation came another twenty years of "Life Readings," which explored the lives of living individuals and historical figures, bringing together in one multicolored New Age skein the teachings of Western and Eastern mysticism and spirituality. Cayce's teachings continued to influence my life for several years and even now a return to his life and insights serves as a reminder of humankind's extraordinary abilities.

Sometime in early 1978, I was invited to a lecture describing the work of the Findhorn Community. Findhorn was a prototype spiritual community that, by the time of this lecture, found itself in a central place in the international New Age movement. Located in northeast Scotland near an obscure fishing village close to the North Sea, it became a refuge for Peter and Eileen Caddy, their companion, Dorothy Maclean, and their three sons. After a number of comfortable years managing a nearby hotel, Peter Caddy, the chief supporter of the group, found himself out of work, on the dole, and all of them living in a trailer in the Findhorn Bay Caravan Park.

To supplement a meager income, the group decided to grow a vegetable garden despite decidedly inhospitable gardening conditions. Their faith and confidence was supported by a history of spiritual discipline that allowed the development of an inner life of contact with spiritual sources. They were, in fact, able in meditation to "receive communications from a source identifying itself as 'the God within.'" They found they were able to contact the "beings" or "devas" who personified the forces of nature and receive instructions on how to provide the optimum physical environment for each specie of plant.

The initial flourishing of that garden was so spectacular that it attracted the attention of many people in Britain and other parts of the world. Some of the visitors who identified with the spiritual relationship of the garden and the gardeners stayed, and the Findhorn Community was born. Slowly, from this modest beginning, the community evolved from one focused on the production of the garden to one focused on its hidden energies. Knowledge about the community seeped out through the written and spoken accounts of individuals who had personal contact with it.

David Spangler and his associate, Myrtle Glines, were among those who heard impressive reports of Findhorn and the "elves, fairies and angelic" beings recruited to help in the magical garden. Spangler and Glines had been exploring methods of integrating different psychological and spiritual levels of consciousness for enhancing creativity and transformation. Although they sensed an identity with these Findhorn rumors, they were looking elsewhere for the next stage of their work, and they had no intention of traveling to Scotland. Despite their intentions however, circumstances conspired to open a window of opportunity for a three-day visit.

What they found there was precisely what they had sought in Europe but until then had not found. Spangler writes in his book, *Revelation: the Birth of a New Age*, of "a developing community where the sense of cocreative contact with other dimensions of life and the presence of a spiritual and integrative energy was stronger than any other place we had ever visited."[3] They remained at Findhorn for a number of years in contact with a "strong presence" that identified itself as "Limitless Love and Truth."[4] Spangler confesses to being a reluctant "channel" or "medium" but acknowledged this knowledge came through him too insistently to be ignored.

These transmissions described the direction and vision of a New Age, the age of Aquarius, in which the spiritual attunement with higher guiding powers would more and more be available to people everywhere. The role of Findhorn in this new period was to establish communities showing people how this attunement could be accomplished. Spangler's book contains most of these transmissions. This book and the general Findhorn experience impacted my life in the oddest way; it came to my attention at the time my material world was again in crisis and it supported me in that crisis with spiritual guidance and psychological protection in a way I could never have predicted.

My job termination took place as scheduled and I found myself once again out of work, in a situation similar to many years earlier with no diminution of my family responsibilities. In some ways my situation was even worse. Eight years older, I was now in my later fifties. I lost this job after only six months, whereas I had had a solid history of employment in the previous situation. It would require an adroit explanation to a new employer to account for this. But rather than the feelings of depression and despair that accompanied the previous crisis, my emotional state was almost of exhilaration, not because I was losing my job—I understood fully the implications of that—but because of my reaction to the loss. As the traumatic event of termination took place, simultaneously unfolding in my awareness was a cascade of contradictory yet positive feelings.

The termination interview seemed to be of greater emotional

trauma for my supervisor and the Human Resource manager than it was for me. I know there will be those who would chide me for my naivete (should I be comforting them?), but they seemed to be genuinely distressed by the difficult position in which I found myself. We were all aware, as they outlined the benefits they were providing, this could have serious consequences for me as I was not being laid off for lack of work. Would I be able to receive Unemployment Insurance, for example? And how would I explain my dismissal?

From my side, I began to realize a growing sense of freedom and independence. Freedom because I was leaving work that in its latter stages was causing me stress and discomfort, and independence because on some level I sensed I did not need even the modicum support my now former employers offered. These feelings seemed to emerge and grow at the time of the interview. Indeed, to recount a minor miracle, there was no negative reaction or sense of insecurity at all.

Rather, I began to realize that my spiritual practice, far removed on the surface from those esoteric New Age teachings and practices in which I immersed myself over the past number of months, actually put me in harmony with the forces these esoteric teachings described. To put it as succinctly as possible: the practice of Transcendental Meditation, although arising as it does from an ancient tradition of Vedic Masters, permitted me to drink deeply from a source of powerful spiritual sustenance. The experiences these teachings portrayed found a deep resonance within me, and I was confident that whatever developed in the next period of time would be supportive and beneficial for me and my family.

This new mode of realization and its emotional consequence developed as part of my interior life. My early negative attempts to discuss those innermost events convinced me that these "bizarre" New Age thoughts better be kept well closeted. Still, their effects were inspiring. I conducted all my necessary activities with a sense of well-being. I went about the business of finding a new job feeling I was living in a benign universe that meant me no harm. I felt so much at ease and secure, in fact, that I went on a TM residence course for a weekend, uncharacteristically spending money at a critical, belt-tightening time.

As fanciful and "other-wordly" as all this seems, these spontaneous expectations of support from nature came to fruition. Shortly after I came back from the TM weekend, a friend and neighbor suggested I see his supervisor as his department was looking for a person and my skills could be useful. Although the interview revealed their needs and my experience were only peripherally compatible, our rapport was so good that the supervisor decided to find a place for me. My fears about explaining why I lost my other job were unfounded. When I told my prospective boss that despite my best efforts I could not satisfy my former supervisor, he responded with perfect understanding; it turns out he had also worked for the same man and he also could not satisfy him, and he also was terminated.

I originally thought the concept of "support of nature" was exemplified by getting that ill-fated job. In fact, of course, it was expressed in being exposed to a completely new way of understanding my place and function in the world through the people I met and new worlds discovered. The lesson of that experience, obviously, is that in spiritual matters as well as mundane, hindsight provides the clearest vision. Spiritual growth, however, is no less uplifting and valuable for all that. So it is with this perfect vision I recognize the harmonious forces of nature that steered me to the best job I ever had in my long working life, at a time I most needed a protected employment environment.

This new company experienced all the needs and requirements of any industrial organization facing competition and other market forces. Yet it had a strong social awareness as well, reaching out to the handicapped community for employees and supporting a family-type atmosphere. My department was especially supportive, and over the years provided understanding for my spiritual and practical needs. Thus, when I needed time off to pursue advanced spiritual techniques in a residential program, they gave me the needed two weeks off and paid me as well.

Years later, when a reorganization took place and my function was eliminated, I was scheduled to lose my job. I found out later that efforts were made to find other work for me but to no avail. The new Engineering Manager was adamant, I was to be let go. The very morning of my last day I later discovered, for reasons still "unknown," he had a change of heart, and new work was found for me. This new position carried me through my final working years, allowing me to remain the economic center of my family and, no less important, permitting my wife and me to accumulate retirement savings.

Approximately three years later, for whatever economic or management reasons, the company's viability was seriously impaired, and it became the victim of a hostile takeover that removed its founding and operating management and altered the nature of its work environment completely. This came at precisely the time I reached full retirement age, and I was able to retire with a small but significant pension. That, along with our savings largely accumulated in the years of work with this company, and Social Security, permitted my wife and me to retire comfortably in relative security. That confluence of emotions—the sense of security, of freedom, of independence, of "being in the flow"—that I enjoyed and trusted in that crisis period nine years before turned out to be fully justified, although on any rational level they could easily have been dismissed as flights of fancy.

This amazing kaleidoscope of images and impressions, hardly to be called ideas, certainly not the mental constructs of a rational consciousness, did not replace my normal common sense view of reality, nor did it affect the daily decision making forced on me by my myriad householder roles. But it did allow this decision making to take place in an emotional environment much more characterized by a calmness and sense of confidence. This state of mind never palled on me and because of that timeless freshness, as awareness of it surfaced, I can only speak or write of it as waves of bliss suffusing my consciousness. In time, an integration took place such that the division between the rational and nonrational—that is, sensory-based and intuitive knowledge—dissolved into one.

Clearly there was nothing in my personal history that would have led me to believe I would accept such a totally idealistic way of looking at the world and my place in it. I was consciously grounded in a materialistic worldview. The influences of my early intellectual life formed by early twentieth-century Marxism remain with me to this very day. Despite the modern discrediting of Marxist-based political and economic systems, I had always found the dialectical materialistic approach to the material world valid and helpful.

But I realized almost immediately, at the onset of experience flowing from meditation, that there was no way to accommodate a metaphysically based worldview with my gross materialistic habit of thinking. Despite this realization I felt reluctant to discard a system of ideas with which I so closely identified. In many ways, and for many years, these ideas had determined how I thought of myself and my place in the world.

I was well aware of Maharishi's insistence that the practice of TM was not a religion, nor in conflict with any religious teaching, that it required no lifestyle change, that it challenged no philosophy. Nevertheless, some time elapsed before the recognition dawned that no reconciliation was necessary, and I am sure it was more intuitive then than on the level I presently understand it. I now recognize I was comparing the validity of two different systems of thought. Like two religions, comparing the value of one teaching and another is useless since both depend on faith, but accommodation is found by transcending the teaching to a higher spiritual level. The Vedic dictum, "knowledge is structured in consciousness," the slogan of the educational institutions founded by Maharishi, establishes the context for this new way of looking at everything.

It is not knowledge in words and ideas, new or old, sensory or nonsensory-based, that makes life and spiritual practice meaningful; rather, it is the spiritual practice itself, the new level of consciousness it produces, that makes this knowledge meaningful and that gives it substance. Thus, I found in all those esoteric schools and expressed wisdom, ancient and modern, scientific and humanist, something I could connect with on an experiential level, needing no expression to "know" it. As my practice continued, new teachers and teachings entered my life, but the lesson of these first few years was, I felt, thoroughly learned: no matter with what bewildering array of knowledge or intellectual conflict one is confronted, awareness of an unshakable center, the awareness reached through meditation, transcends and resolves all problems and questions.

CHAPTER SEVEN

The Blessings I

I *began to settle into a new mode of functioning based on the "unshak-able center."* Previously, I described the waves of joy and well-being that arose spontaneously accompanied by a sense of confidence and satisfaction. These emotions that were once euphoric almost became mundane. Nevertheless, I was still visited periodically by feelings of foreboding and unease that I had long thought gone, and it was always an unexpected shock when they reappeared.

These negative feelings commenced early in my spiritual journey and I characterized them then as St John's "Dark Night of the Soul." But with the passage of time and the accumulation of experience, greater clarity emerged regarding the nature of these "warring" states of consciousness. The two qualities of awareness were distinct, and when I shifted between them it was as if I crossed a threshold separating an area of my perception characterized by intense negative emotions to an area defined as settled, calm, peaceful with no emotional involvement. Yet this was not a mechanical separation, as if an opaque barrier was set up; in either circumstance, contact with the other was never lost, and this experience of emotional freedom was so profound it transformed the nature of all subsequent grief or sorrow that entered my life.

This juxtaposition of mental functioning became established as a pattern in my life for many years. Negativity would often arise spontaneously, although also at times from external distress, with its typical sensations of dread, sorrow, depression, fear and general anxiety. I now became acquainted with the meaning of the term "free floating anxiety," although I was not to hear this expression itself until some years later, as this condition would often simply arise unbidden and unwanted. As it arose so it would dissolve, and when dissolved it left no trace, as no trace of a ripple is left in the evening calm of a country pond.

My new place of employment, the one from which I would eventually retire, was also the one that would provide the environment for the next phase of my spiritual growth. It was there that I began to understand how growth and transformation are made manifest in the context of living one's life. Though changes in function and ability take place on all levels, they are often clearest in human relationships where emotions are involved. I began to realize a new style of behavior and thinking in my interaction with coworkers and supervisors. This was especially noticeable in the fresh start I made as I entered an unfamiliar relationship without the set of preconceptions and expectations that usually stem from a history of people working together.

I had noticed certain positive changes appear in my general attitude and behavior in my previous work places. I knew on an abstract level, like most people know, that feelings of envy, suspicion, unjust treatment, and frustration at work often lead to anger and occupational discontent. Unhappiness at work—the fate of so many people—likely stems more from dysfunctional work relationships than from the nature of the work itself. So I was aware of the shift in my mental disposition with my practice. I became less anxious and envious of someone else's accomplishments, more cooperative and patient working with others, less fretful about receiving credit for my work, more willing to share recognition for accomplishments.

It was not that these attributes were formerly lacking in my behavior and consciousness. Indeed, I think most people would have thought I was a "nice guy," an expression I would have appreciated hearing. But where these qualities were sometimes forced, and their opposite repressed, they now developed spontaneously out of a growing sense of self-assurance. I felt a diminished need to prove myself, to outperform, or to acquire more prestige. Yet at the same time I felt a growing confidence that my work would make a contribution to the overall effort and be appreciated.

I started my new job, then, buoyed by this deepening awareness and looking forward to its fresh expression in a new start. The work was novel in many respects. The duties I was primarily hired for, checking electronic engineering documentation and schematic diagrams, were not being generated in any quantity at the time, so I was reassigned to checking mechanical drawings. The anomaly of this situation is clear when one realizes the normal track to this position requires technical schooling, apprenticeship, and several years of mechanical drawing experience. I had none of this. I needed to learn a new system of engineering specifications, mechanical tolerances, hardware sizes and nomenclature, sheet metal fabrication and related subjects. What I found particularly difficult was the visualization of three-dimensional objects from a two-dimensional drawing, a skill in which I had no background.

Nevertheless, from the beginning I felt at ease. Normally, in this situation, I would have been apprehensive, tense, uncomfortable. Yet, that general positive attitude described above carried over into the early days and weeks and months of my new job. I enjoyed going to work and enjoyed feeling the confidence that pervaded my day. But this calmness had a more important function than to simply make me feel good, which, of course, is no small blessing in itself. The profound sense of security I was living with permitted me to reveal levels of ignorance about myself; that is, to expose a personal vulnerability not easily displayed and that I would have otherwise tried to hide. This allowed me to seek help and guidance I might not have sought in the past. I felt this spiritual support corresponded with the support from most of my fellow workers who, I thought, did everything they could to nurse me through that early period.

I was not that far removed from those qualities I had always thought of as necessary for survival: suspicion, workplace cliques, self-promotion, the fear and hiding of mistakes, the universal need to cover one's backside; to name a few aspects of the cultural environment of so many organizations. On some level I always knew these were destructive attributes, but like the destructive emotions I lived with and fought to overcome all my life, they were so much a part of my identity I could not have imagined life without these feelings.

But I encountered them in myself and others from new levels of involvement and understanding. I recognized their presence in my consciousness, but I recognized also my personal freedom from them. From the status of equanimity I was then enjoying, they had the same psychological force as loosened or untied bindings would have had on my physical body; the feelings are present but easily cast aside.

This is not to say there was a miraculous transformation in our department and these long-ingrained, negative habits disappeared because of my presence. Nor, indeed, can it be said these traits were even recognized by most people as something other than normal functioning. But on a personal level, at least, I found myself unconstrained to enter into those negative relationships, euphemized as office politics, which remains a plague in virtually all business organizations.

I was quite conscious of the advantages this state of mind conferred. The amount of energy wasted and the level of stress endured in continual scheming can only be appreciated when one is free of it. To be part of a social group, then, and to be able to resist its destructive influences without generating hostility, enjoying respect from competing factions, being able to play a reconciling role at times (especially for a person such as me who did it so poorly) was a truly affecting experience.

To do this easily, spontaneously, without guile or forethought, was, I recognized, the material manifestation of spiritual growth. This recognition invariably arose as an introspective afterthought, and it led to the joyous understanding that transcendence in meditation, which was automatic and natural, had its counterpart in transcendence in activity. Thus, ordinary daily intercourse acquires spiritual dimensions when it links one to his or her internal self.

This is not to say I was living in a personal, continuously idyllic state. On the contrary, this was a time when the roller coaster pattern of emotional peaks and valleys became a constant part of my life. As night followed day, a peak experience would be succeeded by a period of familiar ordinary consciousness subject to the anxiety and petty concerns that plagued my pre-meditating life. The transformation itself from one level to another—the word "level" is a good representation of how I thought of it—was clear, but the duration of each period would vary considerably. Although I never tried to find a direct correspondence, I am sure now that much of the change depended on the amount of stress and rest in my life at the time.

This mode of being and functioning was clearly more constructive and satisfying than anything I had known before starting TM. Indeed, there were reminders of this every day. I soon learned, however, I was a poor judge of any correlation between how I perceived myself (that is, the content of my emotions at any particular time) how others saw me and the actual reality of my state of mind. This was brought home to me one day when my work partner confided to me that the quality he first saw in me, and most admired the day I started work, was the air I had of "being at home." Because he was a person who found new social situations very stressful, he was particularly struck by my appearance of complete ease.

He made this remark as I informed him I was preparing to go to a TM weekend residence course and would be taking off early that afternoon. I had never mentioned my meditating practice to him before. He told me he had attended TM lectures in the past but was singularly unimpressed. Yet somehow he immediately connected my meditative practice with my behavior. I was genuinely surprised at his observation. This was the first time anyone had so clearly voiced, from a truly innocent perspective, this so deeply felt emotion. This sense of being "at ease" was so internalized, and recognition of it so personal and satisfying, that the idea of purposefully projecting it, even were that possible for someone else to recognize, would somehow violate it. If this was the first time I heard this remark it was not the last, and each time I would feel the same sense of surprise. But it also evoked a pleasing confirming effect, bringing this internal reality to my outer conscious awareness. A happy consequence of this incident was my partner's subsequent decision to become a meditator.

This almost ideal working environment had a life of its own, and like all life was subject to inevitable change. As new supervision and personnel came and went, a marked altering of a formerly benign atmosphere took place. For unknown reasons, a sharp deterioration in supervisory staff took place with a leadership nadir of sorts being reached with the person who was to become my direct supervisor. This individual suffered from a paranoia and mental incompetence so extreme that he was finally fired. But before that took place the good working conditions and high morale of an entire department were destroyed. For me, personally, it became a serious crisis.

I began spending weeks and months at a time dealing with the most egregious expressions of suspicion, religious fanaticism and just plain ignorance I had ever encountered in one person. If there were any spiritual arrogance engendered in me by the previous period, it was wiped out by the onset of the stressful period I entered then. Over the years I had built up a reservoir of goodwill with many friends and from these I received sympathy and emotional support, but because of overall management indifference there was little else anyone could do. At this point I fell into a downward spiraling desperate situation and I felt completely isolated.

During this period the ideas of reincarnation and karma again surfaced as a new approach to understanding. Combined with the experience of new psychic dimensions uncovered in meditation, this gross assault on my mental well-being made it easy to latch on to anything that promised help. Meditation, then, intertwined with the ideas of past life influences, became a powerful coping tool. On a deep internal level that familiar central core of silence remained. But it was a small light spot surrounded by a field of darkness, often only a flicker, threatening to extinguish in the face of the emotional maelstrom generated by this dilemma. So when the idea arose that this confusing and despairing situation could be the result of a karmic debt incurred in a past life and was now being redeemed, the thought that this debt would soon be gone entered my mind like the flash of a lighthouse beacon.

From my reading and contact with other meditators over the years, I was well aware of these ideas. I knew they were central to Vedic teaching and peripherally part of Christianity, Judaism and other major religions. They are, however, alien to the Western psychological tradition, which is generally limited to a scientific, material approach to mental phenomenon. Until now, I assumed a curious, nonjudgmental attitude to these ideas. Maharishi touches on reincarnation and karma in his two main philosophical books, *Maharishi Mahesh Yogi on the Bhagavad-Gita*, and *The Science of Being and the Art of Living*, but there was no encouragement in the meditation centers to discuss or relate these concepts to modern physiology and psychology, or use them to explain the results and benefits of meditation.

It was these ancient Eastern ideas, however, that provided me with a crystal-clear, practical and satisfying explanation for my present position and a way out of it. With no thought or intellectual evaluation, I simply accepted the notion that what was being inflicted on me was the result of an action I committed sometime in a past life, and I was paying for it now. The most comforting and beautiful aspect of this idea was that, once repaid, these misdeeds would vanish and would no longer impact on my life. I have no illusions about how outlandish these concepts appear to most people who form my intimate and casual social milieu, including many fellow meditators. For me, these beliefs are intellectually indefensible and certainly not ones I can promote, even if I had any intention of doing so. But the concepts were so consistent with the reality of my life at the time, that they easily became integrated into a continuously developing worldview.

As bizarre as the concepts of reincarnation and karma may seem to be, they fit hand in glove into the actual events that finally resolved this negative period of my life. Abruptly as this situation began, it ended. The Engineering Department reorganization was swift and complete with no position left untouched. The most important effect for me was the immediate dismissal of my "nemesis." His resignation was asked for and received the same day, and he was unceremoniously escorted out of the building. My sense of isolation dissolved instantly as people on all levels indicated they had, in fact, recognized my problem. It was at this point that the karmic implications of the experience emerged and fixed in my mind a fresh and exciting approach to all future negativity.

As this person was being escorted out of the building, I felt a miasma lift from the atmosphere dispelling the heaviness that so long accompanied me at work. But it was not an exhilaration or excitement that I felt; it was a quiet satisfaction that an ordeal was over and the proper order of things was being restored. I had no anger nor enmity toward anyone, rather an overwhelming feeling that something was finished, complete, without residue. As intense as the experience was when it was occurring, little impression of it remained when it was over. I do not mean it faded in time; I mean no time and no mental effort were needed before the entire experience became a memory without emotional substance.

I was aware I was functioning on a different psychological, or to use a more inclusive word, "spiritual" level. As I look back now, I vaguely remember when the thought that an emotional flatness was beginning to pervade my being. It took a strange form in its earliest period, in a flattening out of my sense of joy. Pleasure at my successes or the successes of loved ones no longer produced the highs to which I was accustomed. Perversely however, I could suffer the pangs of failure. I knew this was a result of meditation. But because the benefits of meditation were so generally positive, I was confident that this experience, although confusing at the moment, was also beneficial. This intuition was proven correct by the quiescent nature of my reaction to the end of that year-long traumatic event. I glimpsed clearly then what it means to live completely in the present; the past loses its hold and the future holds no fear. This was the delicious taste of life in freedom.

As this new understanding illuminated my relationships at work, it simultaneously provided remarkable insights in what is probably the most intractable of all human relationships, that of the family. No relationships have deeper roots than those of parents, children and siblings. All cultures develop formative myths revealing psychological and spiritual depths that are a complex melange of jealousy, affection, love and hatred. And in modern psychology, there are no personal problems (for some, societal problems as well) that do not have their origins in family relationships. The most recent theories, extending the cause of these personality anomalies—positive and negative—to genetics only emphasize their deep-seated place in the deep recesses of humankind. Yet the self-development psychological theories pioneered by Maslow, the knowledge of Eastern teachings, and the experience of Eastern spiritual practice, provide the experiential evidence that even these seemingly intransigent problems can be dissolved.

My personal family history was no exception to this universal condition. I was twenty-six years old when my father died, he was in his early fifties, and I remember the confused mixture of sadness and release when I heard of it. The sense of release came from the recognition that my futile search for his esteem and respect came to an end, and sadness because the opportunity to finally receive that blessing also had ended. I never pursued a goal, it seemed, which he thought had merit and I rebelled against his attempt to script my life to satisfy his desires. This relationship saddened us both. And despite my resentment and guilt-laden hate, I sensed his love and concern for me, yet my efforts to please him by doing what I thought he wanted only made things worse for both of us. It is, I believe, only in these inextricable family relationships that this unique set of love and hate passions can arise.

I was the middle of three sons. It was of little help that my older brother faced the same problems with our father that I did. It was, in fact, an added burden when he would mirror our father's attitude, and in some ways it was worse because I had for him the typical awe and respect due to older brothers. My mother was my only ally in this continual conflict, but she was able to offer only emotional support in what was a traditional patriarchal home. The most difficult situation was my Dad's rapport with my younger brother. All the attention, support and affection I so deeply desired and so sorely missed he gave to him.

I know there was no nefarious plan in this, of course. This brother was naturally the kind of person my father was able to identify with and appreciate. He wanted us, my older brother and me, to be just like him, and it frustrated him terribly that we could not. But as this sibling's successes and relatively smooth transition from boyhood, through adolescence, and into adulthood took place within the family, my situation was a steadily deteriorating one. The more he was held up as an example I should follow, predictably, the more my bitterness toward all of them increased.

Love, affection, support, respect and appreciation are vital human needs, and, ideally, for normal personality development, they should first be acquired within the immediate family struc- ture. Failing this, if these qualities are to be attained at all, they have to be obtained in external circumstances. This was the case for me, and the legacy it left for the next three decades of my life was a schizoid disposition that functioned one way in my role as husband, father, employee and social being, and in another as son and sibling. The more or less successful achievements of my life were unable to modify the condescending attitudes always present when I was with my brothers and mother. Indeed, the bane of my existence was the reversion to these childhood relations whenever a family gathering took place. The paradox was easy to understand but impossible to resolve: the ideal solution would be to not expose myself to the trauma of these meetings, but the desire to achieve recognition and appreciation from them was so strong that I did not want to destroy that possibility by giving up contact.

When my mother said to me one day, after we were forced into a closer one-on-one relationship, "meditation must be good for you, you're not so sensitive anymore," she recognized in my external bearing what I began to sense internally. What I was accused of, as being too "sensitive," was my response to the "constructive criticism" or "good-natured teasing" she and especially my younger sibling would offer. In family gatherings I was always on the defensive, explaining and justifying everything I did. The way I lived was, to be sure, different in many ways than theirs and perhaps justified their attitude in their minds. But at almost every meeting I would find myself being provoked into responding to criticism and teasing, often inappropriately, often stupidly.

I usually reacted to these events with as much anger at myself as at them. Try as I might, each time I prepared for a visit, to steel myself to resist provocations, it was usually to no avail. It is, indeed, possible I may not have wanted to resist, so complicated and hidden are these emotional bindings, and so futile were the attempts. The first inkling that there was a breaking up of this mountain of congealed stress occurred while driving home from a visit with my mother and brother. I was almost at the end of an hour's drive when I realized the internal dialogue I inevitably conducted about our visits was not taking place. Our meetings never ended for me when I left their physical presence; usually I would mull the arguments over and over in my mind, but this time that did not happen.

Moreover, I realized this was consistent with another mental phenomenon I was becoming increasingly aware of. All my life my mind was filled with thoughts. These were not only the directed thoughts involved in solving problems, understanding ideas or the nature of the world, which one would believe is the purpose of thinking, but the incessant storm of mental activity. They were as much a part of my life as breathing, and as little recognized, even when deliberately pushed aside when they insinuated themselves into periods of concentration and focus. This was so naturally a part of my waking state consciousness that I could never have imagined that quieting one's mind meant a mind without thoughts.

I had been experiencing intermittent episodes of this quieting for very short periods. If I were to judge I would say they lasted a few moments or seconds, but long enough for me to notice them. In a typical case, when looking at a scene I would be aware of the scene but I would also be aware of the I doing the looking, with no extraneous thoughts. Logically, then, if my eyes were closed I would simply be aware of the I. This latter experience was somewhat familiar to me because it was not uncommon in meditation.

If this situation had been described to me, and likely it had been, I could not have understood the explanation. How can one describe the psychological effects of a mind not beset by this uncontrollable river of thoughts without the actual taste of it? The convergence of these sporadic mental silences with that long, peaceful ride home established a new foundation for knowledge. And it also began a complete transformation of a set of relationships that had their origins fixed in childhood, and which burrowed deeper and deeper over a lifetime.

In a classical example of Jungian synchronicity, I learned to meditate at roughly the same time as the onset of a great family tragedy affecting all of us, especially my mother, who was beginning her eighty-first year. My older brother just entered the terminal period of lung disease and my younger brother, for his part, was recovering from a serious heart bypass operation. Not long after my older brother died, the other's condition persuaded him to retire very early from his successful business and move to an area more congenial to his health. The two pillars of support my aging mother depended on were gone, and the only person left to shore up her increasingly dependent state, me, was the one she had the least confidence in.

By the time she made that observation about my "sensitivity" we had achieved a intimacy we never could have thought possible. Old habits die hard, so the criticisms, demands, disapprovals, and her long-practiced expertise of instilling guilt continued, but for the most part my different state of mind blunted the worst of it. She recognized this and became interested in my spiritual practice, with uncharacteristic astuteness, I thought, recognizing its role in making a new relationship possible. Little by little we began to explore areas of mutual interest outside the recriminations and fault finding that ordinarily occupied our time together, and a real friendship began to develop allowing us to reveal more vulnerable aspects of ourselves to each other. A major turning point occurred when I described a dream to her I had about my father in what I now recognize as a mutual spiritual epiphany.

I am not a person for whom dreams had great significance. Over the course of many years, however, I experienced a recurring dream of being lost, which gradually left its influence. While the details of this dream would change, its basic theme was always a knowing where I wanted to go, how to get there, yet an inexplicable inability to do so. Its meaning still perplexes me as I find it difficult to correlate it with my waking state activities. Other than that, my dreams receive little attention. But this one about my father was so intense it involved all my senses as if I were awake. When I was a child he used to rub his unshaven cheek against mine in an affectionate, teasing way. I dreamed that he was doing this again. There was a characteristic feeling and smell and a typical chuckle about this event that came flooding into my consciousness. I had an overwhelming sense of his presence. We were in a semi-embrace and I felt we shared an undiluted love for each other. There was no sense of bitterness or conflict, simply pure acceptance. The image, or vision, or whatever the form was that I embraced, slowly started to fade as I entered that amorphous state before full awakening. I cannot describe the depth of silence I felt as I came awake in the quiet of the early morning. But it was in this silence that those destructive and hateful feelings poisoning my life for so many years dissolved. Never again did I think of him with other than love and affection and great understanding as my own fatherhood matured.

I could not have given my mother a greater gift than the recounting of this dream. It was a source of great distress for her that her sons, especially me, expressed such bitterness and alienation toward him, and she could not break through these attitudes. She could acknowledge our feelings but she loved him deeply and always knew he loved us; her only defense of him was we did not understand the harsh difficulties of his life, and it frustrated her that we could not understand how our relationship saddened him as much as it estranged us. This dream, then, was the shared epiphany that created new bonds between us and one which colored the rest of our lives together.

As my mother passed her mid-eighties, she could no longer live alone. Our two lives now became as inseparably intertwined as they were at my birth, only this time I was the shelterer, the protector, the nourisher, the arbiter of her future. Aside from the physical and psychological infirmities she increasingly suffered, she lived in a part of the city now drug-ridden and violent. It became a frightening experience for me to visit her in the neighborhood in which we were born and raised and where she spent most of her life. All her lifelong friends were gone and her new neighbors and friends, helpful and caring as many of them were, lived in a different world speaking a strange language. Without me, she was alone and frightened.

The time of crisis finally arrived when her well-being and care forced aside my family and job concerns and became the over-whelming focus of my life. On the surface, I faced an impossible situation. She could not stay where she was. If I brought her to live with me, as she was begging me to do, it would destroy our family life. And she vowed to resist moving to a home for seniors with all her breath. Despite her resistance, to please me she agreed to inspect and interview the local Isabella Home. If there was any place she would agree to go to it would be this one; she knew it fairly well, often visiting friends there. Although nonsectarian, it had a large Jewish population that shared her life and her memo-ries, and it was highly acclaimed for the care it showed its residents. She knew its reputation, which was confirmed by her visit. I knew it was the only viable solution.

My spirits soared when we left after our tour and she indicated it might not be so bad if she did go there after all. And as high as they soared, that was how low they plummeted when in almost the next instant she changed her mind, telling me I "would have to call the police to get her there." But despite her continuous ambivalence, I had no choice but to pursue this goal. As this crisis situation unfolded, I became aware of a deep and clear sense of invulnerability, that my very being, soul, essence, all valid terms, were untouched by these events. It was not that there was a reve-lation of some great knowledge—actually that came many years later—or that I was touched by some divine force, although some could see it as such; it was that on the deepest level I sensed there was no problem. As the crisis unfolded, I started to deal with it on an issue-by-issue basis with confidence that each "problem" would be resolved.

At work, I told my supervisor what was happening. He received my everlasting appreciation when he told me to attend to my personal needs and do what company work I could around them. For all practical purposes, my office became "headquarters" with unlimited telephone use, absolutely indispensable for our needs since I was in Connecticut and all communication was with New York City institutions. I called Isabella House to get the paper work started. We had established my mother's financial status, and they told me she was already evaluated and found acceptable for their minimum care facility. They would put her on their waiting list but we must be prepared for a long wait; they could not estimate a time when a room would be available.

We started to systematically prepare her to accept relocation, especially as her personal situation deteriorated. She was not cooking for herself so my wife had been preparing and separately packaging meals to supplement the one Meals-on-Wheels lunch she would get each day. We would both come down and spend weekends with her, helping to clean and cook. We had to individually wrap her daily medication, and still she would forget to take it. I would receive calls at work every day from a neighbor or the building superintendent for one crisis or another. Our lives were essentially on hold as they revolved around the needs of my mother.

Horrendous as this sounds, it was these crises that exposed the promise and depths of my spiritual practice. I found each situation was a singular event that existed only as long as the event existed. That is, before the onset of whatever was to occur there was repose without anticipation or worry. While each event demanded primary attention, when the event ended the mind once again entered repose. The unruffled ocean gives rise to the wave, then the wave dissolves into the unruffled ocean. This state of mind is often most clearly revealed in hindsight, yet is no less appreciated or important for that. That it exists at all gives credence to the promise, if not yet fulfilled, of continuous life in bliss and freedom. What matters most to those of us struggling with these householder problems is that just the taste of that level of life, though it brings us only a hairbreadth out of ignorance, is enough to free us from the bondage of despair and helplessness.

Once again my intuitive confidence in the benign forces I somehow automatically contact in my meditation practice was justified. About ten days after my mother was put on the waiting list, Isabella called and told me they had a place for her. Within the next week she was moved to a safe and secure environment where she remained for the rest of her life, dying after a short illness at ninety-three years old. It was not easy to finally convince her to move, nor can I say she was completely happy there. But she was never really happy anywhere.

In my earliest fantasies I envisaged a time when my family would accord me the respect and appreciation, as well as the deference, earned by important achievements and financial success. How, I would imagine, the satisfaction that would bring! Alas, important achievements, at least from a worldly perspective of financial success, continue to elude me, but the most delicious irony is that they no longer have relevance to my needs. These fantasies exist no longer; they have all come to fruition, not out of the realization of transitory external needs, but out of the realization of the depths of my own being, my Self.

I feel a peace with my older brother and father such that I cannot associate any sense of bitterness or rancor with their memories. On the contrary, as I think of them I often feel a sense of joy, not only because the joy and pleasure we had once given each other is no longer hidden by that destructive mutual enmity, but also because the thought reminds me that those destructive qualities are no longer part of my life. Before her death, my mother made clear that her mind now understood what her heart so long desired. In her eyes I became a real *mensch*, a Jewish word that is translated to mean a responsible and mature adult, a person who can be counted on. We found a peace together that sanctified our relationship.

With my mother's death, my younger brother remains the last physical tie to the family into which I was born. Our ongoing living relationship reflects, in its entirety, the feelings I have toward the others. I know this is true from my side and I have no doubt any longer that it is true from his. He was unable to lift a finger to help our mother at the time of her greatest need, and his fears for her represented a tremendous burden for him. I cannot imagine what would have happened to him, or to her, were I not there and able to care for her. It was during that period, little by little, I began to receive his respect and appreciation.

For my part, in the supreme irony of spiritual growth, all sense of personal satisfaction in the results of my efforts were softened by my realization that the ultimate author of these efforts was on a nonego, nonpersonal level of reality. Consequently, there was no need to cut through any hostility, or to "get even" for past affronts. Indeed, those, real and imagined, no longer existed. My brother and I now enjoy a mutually uplifting, supporting and loving relationship, sharing family joys, accomplishments, trials and sorrows.

CHAPTER EIGHT
The Teachers II

*T*he need to explain observed phenomenon is so compelling in human nature that the explanation only needs some connection with what is being observed, even if miniscule, for us to accept it. For most of our history, and much of our prehistory, our ancestors understood their material and psychological world in terms completely alien to the modern scientific view. The treasured mythology of the world's people attest to this. Since the emergence of the Newtonian mechanical worldview in the 17th century, there has been a systematic and overpowering ideological struggle to reduce this beautiful human legacy to the level of airy, impractical mental exercise. Indeed, the very reservoir of this knowledge has been declared nonexistent, and it is said the only valid information about the world is that obtained by our senses, which by default limits the world to its material nature.

I accepted this philosophy from a very early age, championing this point of view with acquaintances, friends and family. It was therefore an extraordinary reversal of Western intellectual history, exhibited on a personal level, when I preferred, or sought out—or rather realized—a spontaneously emerging explanation for my material and emotional experiences that was better suited for a prescientific age. This situation was not unique with me. With the enormous growth of the meditating population in the 1970s and 1980s, and my growing knowledge of the esoteric teachings of other traditions and their followers, I found kindred spirits everywhere.

I was not estranged from Western scientific thinking because of this new found knowledge. Nor did these new ideas isolate me from the larger community that did not share them. But they added a dimension to my understanding of the world that was to become the dominant approach to the interpretation of my total experience. The scientific view remains an indispensable tool for dealing with the mundane nature of activity; but more and more as my life unfolds, the revealed wisdom of Eastern and Western sages provides evermore satisfaction as the deeper purposes of existence are uncovered.

Ironically, the man who was responsible for bringing me to this pass was busy translating this wisdom into the scientific language I was finding burdensome and limiting. Early in his contact with the West, Maharishi saw the need to transcribe the Vedic teachings of his Master into the language and concepts of Western man. Consequently, the description of personal evolution from the Eastern tradition, honed over thousands of years of experience, was being recast in terms of blood pressure measurements, brain wave synchrony and hormonal secretions.

As carefully as I perused the psychological and physiological charts, I could not find in them the joy or the irresistible charm I found in the ancient concepts of karma, or past life influences, reincarnation, world masters, spirit guides and other universes inhabited by benign, loving teachers. Nor were the scientific explanations for the reduction in anxiety I felt—the lessening of all kinds of hostility or my increasing sense of well-being—as satisfying, or as empowering, as my sense of contact with a limitless universe. It was not until much later that I came to appreciate the necessity of reconciling modern science with those immemorial

Eastern teachings. And I came to appreciate as well the genius required to accomplish this reconciliation.

One day, I do not remember how or exactly when, a compilation of these esoteric teachings came into my possession. As prepared as I may have thought I was with the unfolding of these ideas in my consciousness, I was not prepared for Baird T. Spalding's five small volumes, *Life and Teaching of the Masters of the Far East.*[1] Spalding was one of a group of eleven Western researchers who visited the "Far East" in 1894 and, in his words, contacted "the Great Masters of the Himalayas." These Masters, or Elder Brothers, he learned, are guiding the destiny of humankind through a great universal brotherhood of those who are able to identify themselves with Universal Law. Human suffering is great and progress is slow, they would say, because this identification has not reached large enough sections of the population. Spalding and the others were permitted to enter into an intimate relationship with these Masters.

There was not a single example of New Age thinking, Vedic teaching or mysticism from any tradition, which I had encountered in the past several years that was not described or demonstrated to Spalding and his party by these Masters. The demonstrations often assumed incredible forms: meetings with a living, physical Jesus and Buddha, astral projection, instant healing and a myriad of "minor" abilities such as levitation, becoming invisible, and tapping into the source of cosmic energy. "The Masters," Spalding says, "accept that Buddha represents the Way to Enlightenment, but they clearly set forth that Christ IS Enlightenment...."[2] These events took place in the late 19th century, and Spalding published his reports in 1924, not sure even then if "the world was ready to hear about them."[3]

Reading this material reminded me of an earlier time in my spiritual journey when I first encountered descriptions of unbelievable abilities by advanced spiritual masters. I felt the same confusion I did then and a little despair. There was a subtle nagging in the back of my mind that these wild reports would somehow nullify the new "truths" I was living by; I could not doubt my experience but the experience and knowledge relationship was shaken. On the basis of my meditation experience, and the results of it in my outer life, I had found comfort and satisfaction in a supernatural explanation of this experience. Now the poison of doubt was doing its work.

The logical extension of this supernatural explanation, which was contained in the teachings of these Far Eastern Masters, involved severing my connections with a conventional worldview, something I was not prepared to do. This intellectual impulse, and it was more impulse than articulation, was analogous to the meditation experience I reported earlier: during meditation, when I thought I was going to leave my body, I became frightened and opened my eyes to abort the "disaster." Similarly now, there was a fear that I was entering an area dissolving a link with a manageable psychological frame of reference. Without the authority of experience or the guidance of a trusted counselor, I could not easily enter this new level of knowledge.

It was about this time another of those meaningful coincidences occurred, which were becoming more and more commonplace. I was invited to a lecture at the house of a Transcendental Meditation teacher whom I had never before met. Ethlyn H. was not typical of TM teachers who were then being trained by Maharishi. For practical reasons, dictated by the needs of the time and the teaching training program, most TM teachers were young, unencumbered by family responsibilities and flexible in their ability to relocate rapidly. For that reason, the largest single group of meditation teachers during the period of TM's greatest expansion, in the mid and late 1970s, were college students or faculty. Meeting Ethlyn was a singular event then, if for no other reason than the obvious differences between her and most other TM teachers.

She was a retired school teacher of indeterminate age. A first impression suggested a woman of advanced years, various people would estimate her age from sixty to eighty years. But as one got to know her, the years tended to melt away, not only because of an intellectual sharpness, but also because of an evident physical vitality. We became friendly after our first meeting, and for the next two years we often traveled together to meetings, courses and lectures. She became an important spiritual guide and mentor to me within this brief time in our relationship. Ethlyn was a private person, and despite the many quiet hours we spent together there was very little I learned of her personal life and history. I was vaguely aware from our conversations that she came to the TM program from a background of other spiritual pursuits, which I believed were grounded in Christianity, but the nature of these spiritual practices or disciplines was never revealed to me. She taught TM in the area in which her retirement community was located, lecturing in local churches and libraries, social meetings and often in private homes. She was a devoted TM teacher, lecturing and teaching according to the desires and instructions of her own teacher, Maharishi.

I immediately found in Ethlyn a person to whom I could reveal my developing spiritual questioning and unease. There was nothing, it seemed, I could say to her with which she was unfamiliar or to which she was unsympathetic. I recited a complete account of the anxiety I was feeling between orthodox TM center teaching and the arcane knowledge coming from all sides and for which I felt so much attraction. We did not talk of these matters in terms of what is true or not; that seemed inappropriate in this context. Rather, as we talked about them I sensed in these teachings a deeper reality, and I thought that through our contact the knowledge became less a function of my mind and more an aspect of my being.

The highlight of this phase of our relationship came when I told her of my reaction to Spalding's "Masters" book. She made no comment about the book itself but mentioned meeting Baird T. Spalding as a young girl when he was a guest in her parent's home. In some strange way this physical connection to Spalding dissolved much of my bothersome questioning about his work. I felt there was a purposeful closing of a circle in which we were all joined. It was not that I found his reports more credible; credibility was not the issue, it was that I found myself much less judgmental regarding them. I realized a new understanding of the concept that knowledge without experience is incomplete, meaningless and without practical significance. This is true of the theoretical knowledge of science, where theory must be validated by experiment, but it is most clearly true of spiritual knowledge, where personal experience is the ultimate authority.

Ethlyn and I parted as cleanly as we came together. One day she was there and one day she was gone. When I could not reach her by telephone, I tried the one friend we had in common in her little community, but she could only tell me Ethlyn was on a trip. It was then I began to realize the nature of our purely teacher and student relationship, important as it may have been to me on many other levels. We simply lost contact. The other TM teachers in the area with whom she interacted, similarly, knew no more about her whereabouts than I did.

One day, on impulse, I called her home, and to my great surprise she was there. She was leaving the area, she told me, and I gathered she was arranging her affairs. She was now part of another spiritual group, not associated with Transcendental Meditation, and she was living with them in a Western state. I was perplexed and curious wanting to understand her thinking about this. But in her typical manner, she simply informed me of her decision in such a way as to indicate that was the end of the conversation. Strangely, aside from the formal mutual well-wishing, we had nothing more to say to each other. The group she is with is fortunate, indeed, to be graced by her presence.

In many of our past conversations I often expressed the need for an "authority" to provide a level of psychological comfort with all the surreal information coming at me from every direction. She never assumed that role of authority but would often indicate that this knowledge was as important and meaningful to her as to me. One day she suggested we attend a lecture given by Charlie Lutes to be held in our area under the auspices of the TM "movement." I never heard of him before but Ethlyn told me he was a founding member of the TM movement in the United States and had worked closely with Maharishi for many years. She thought he would be able to address many of my questions. As I look back at this incident now, I think of it as her way of transferring one of her students into the care of another teacher.

Charles Lutes, or Charlie, as I understand Maharishi was fond of calling him, and how he was known throughout the TM movement, was one of the earliest supporters and leaders of the first organization formed to teach Transcendental Meditation in the United States. The United States organization of the Spiritual Regeneration Movement (SRM) was founded in Los Angeles in 1959 and Charlie soon replaced its first president, Dr. John Hislop. He quickly became Maharishi's chief confidant and organizational assistant during the critical early days of the movement.

As Maharishi was the custodian and dispenser of this ancient Vedic wisdom, extraordinarily able to bring it out to the world, Charlie was the nuts and bolts constructor of this new spiritual Noah's Ark. He bridged the cultural gap between East and West, carried the "deerskin," and likely spent more intimate time with Maharishi than any other American disciple.

When I first met him and heard him speak in the late 1970s, the SRM, of which he was still the head, was by then supplanted by a number of other organizations. These were now identifying and associating TM with Western science and defining spirituality in that context. The SRM and Charlie were still formally part of the TM movement, and Charlie, himself, was a trustee of Maharishi International University (MIU).[4] I do not know when or how this formal relationship with the university and the TM organization finally ended.

Over the years I sensed that many TM teachers were not happy with his identification with the movement as his metaphysical ideas seemed to be at odds with Maharishi's teachings. My spiritual experience and personal feelings then and now, however, lead me to believe Maharishi had less difficulty with Charlie's lectures than they did. Nevertheless, he continues to lecture to groups of devoted followers and even now in his eightieth year maintains (I have been led to believe) a continuing relationship with Maharishi.

But these issues were far from my mind when I entered the crowded university auditorium where the lecture was held. An air of excitement pervaded the room even though most of the attendees had heard him speak before, and for all practical purposes knew what he was going to say. I understand that now as I, too, had continued to attend his lectures over the years and enjoyed the esoteric nature of his message, not for its content so much, but for how it resonated with my growing awareness.

I cannot, after all this time, say explicitly that what I have now integrated into my consciousness in this context came from Charlie Lutes, or Baird Spalding, or any of the multitudinous esoteric sources that stimulated my new understanding. Like the others, Charlie Lutes spoke of spiritual Masters and hierarchies, angels and visions and communication with other realms. The concept of protective spirit guides and the influence of past lives could have come from any of these sources. But it does not matter, because Charlie, like all of them, spoke to my soul, not my head, and it was my soul that responded.

Because of his long and intimate association with Maharishi, he provided the authority I needed to enter this ever-unfolding world with more comfort and confidence. In Charlie's presence I always felt the presence of Maharishi, and he would unfailingly point out that in his person, and as a symbol, Maharishi represented the soul and substance of spiritual masters. In all fairness, I understood how the teaching of Transcendental Meditation in this context would fail to reach large sections of the American population, let alone institutional society such as the schools. But the state of my temperament at the time, arising out of my meditation experience, made this mystical world a powerful and vitalizing reality and lessened the importance of the more rational.

The paradox of mystical literature is that it is a body of work describing an aspect of reality that even its writers regard as ineffable; that is, it cannot be written about. Nonetheless, the literature of transcendence, that condition of human life beyond sensory influence, that place where one touches a universal presence, likely has had more words, oral or written, dedicated to it than any other subject since man's first emergence on the planet. There seems to be a compelling impulse to draw it out of oneself when it is recognized, as those who have felt this presence need to find it in others. For this reason teachers and students of this knowledge have searched and found each other from the beginning of history.

This new dimension of understanding came at exactly the time when my own spiritual development entered an unpredictable new phase. It was a natural progression from Eastern to Western mysticism. Christianity, Judaism and Islam share with Yoga, Buddhism and Taoism, indeed, all traditions, an identical core of mystical experience. Descriptions of this experience from any tradition find a response and agreement from any other, no matter how alien they may seem on the surface. Thus, Jan van Ruysbroeck (1293-1381), writing as a devout medieval Catholic mystic, can speak for all:

> There follows the union *without distinction*. Enlightened men have found within themselves an essential contemplation which is *above reason and beyond reason*, and a fruitive tendency which pierces through every condition and all being, and in which they immerse themselves in a *wayless abyss of fathomless* beatitude where the Trinity of the Divine Persons possess in their nature in the *essential unity*. Behold this beatitude is *so onefold and so wayless* that in it every...*creaturely distinction ceases and passes away*...[5]

Ruysbroeck's words, it was clear to me, shared the characteristics common to the reports from universal mystical sources: "union without distinction," thoughts "above reason and beyond reason," "a wayless abyss" were expressions that resounded with a crystalline brilliance to my inner spirit. And it was these expressions, too, that carried me into a deep appreciation of the essential nature of Christianity and unavoidably into the essential nature of Jesus Christ, as I thought I understood him. To me he became a spiritual Master, a Guru, a teacher, one who could bring humanity from darkness to light, as I felt I was being brought into the light.

This was an extraordinary development personally. I had no traditional or cultural relationship to Christ or Christianity. Even that most tenuous connection, the fact we were both Jews, had no reality. I always thought of myself as part of the Jewish people, but I had no religion and had professed a conscious atheism. This atheism, of course, had by this time been shattered by my meditative experience. But now, once again, a new dimension of this spiritual life stood revealed. I likened it at a later date to entering a new and more inner room in St Teresa's *Interior Castle*,[6] where one progresses room by room to, ultimately, the innermost chamber where one finds Ruysbroeck's "union without distinction."

Spiritual evolution, like historical or biological evolution, once embarked on a specific path, attracts those forces and ideas that tend to maintain its growth on that path. Thus, I now encountered a new world of sacred teaching, the Gnostic Gospels. This new teaching allowed me to appreciate my Eastern-derived Transcendental Meditation practice as an integral part of a natural and universal human desire to reach divine union. I do not remember the sequence in which these ideas based on the life and teachings of Jesus came into my awareness. But sequence does not really matter as knowledge gained latterly often serves to cast new meaning and importance on that gained earlier. Therefore my introduction to the Gnostic Gospels provided a new understanding of and connection to Christian mysticism. But it did not supersede or displace the otherworldly ideas I previously embraced. Rather, it was an enlarging or deepening of one seamless body of knowledge.

The Gnostic Gospels were found in 1945, near the Upper Egypt town of Naj Hammadi, providing additional knowledge of the life and teaching of Jesus. These gospels, which were condemned and excluded from the orthodox gospel selections, threw a powerful light into the shadowy and hidden recesses of early Christian history. Gnostics (from the Greek word, gnosis, meaning those who know) were Christians who denied the literal view that Jesus was resurrected in the flesh. The resurrection, they believed, was a spiritual, not bodily return—one, therefore, that would permit anyone to experience Jesus in his own way and receive the benefits of that experience without the need of clerical intermediaries. Gnostics believed: "self-knowledge is knowledge of God; the self and the divine are identical."[7]

Elaine Pagels quotes the gnostic *Gospel of Thomas* illustrating this concept:

> Jesus said: "I am not your master. Because you have drunk, you have become drunk from the bubbling stream which I have measured out....He who will drink from my mouth will become as I am: I myself shall become he, and the things that are hidden will be revealed to him."[8]

Pagels continues: "Does not such teaching—identity of the divine and human, the concern with illusion and enlightenment, the founder who is presented not as lord, but as spiritual guide—sound more Eastern than Western?"[9] I felt a curious identity with these gnostics as I was drawn to the life and teachings of Jesus on a different level altogether. This contact provided an emotional sustenance such that hearing about him or reading about him as a man or teacher evoked an ardent response and would produce a sense of security, a feeling that all is well with the world. I was drawn to novels about his life, such as the work of Sholem Asch, and felt an eerie relationship to the historical period in which he lived. It was a "nonorthodox" Jesus that I identified with and loved who brought out these feelings, and *The Aquarian Gospel of Jesus the Christ,* that perennial mystical life of Jesus, became a long-time favorite.

Thomas Merton's writings and the writings about him were another source of spiritual inspiration that somehow found its way into my consciousness. I have no recollection of deliberately seeking out this material; I cannot even now remember how I was introduced to it. But I think of it as both a blessing and a catalyst: a blessing for the content of his life and a catalyst because it reinforced this new dimension. I began to understand Christian mysticism as a parallel development in Christian history, primarily in the Catholic Church. The word "catholic" in its Latin origins means "universal, whole, all-inclusive," and it was in the mysticism it generated where these goals were realized. As a non-Christian, I found in the structure, or body, of the Church little of relevance, but I embraced its mystical aspect, or its soul, with the same enthusiasm with which I previously embraced Eastern mysticism.

In a remarkable synchronistic development from a personal point of view, my TM initiation corresponded with an explosion in the 1970s of the teaching of Eastern spiritualism in the United States and, my sense is, in Western Europe. By the latter part of that decade, large numbers of Christians and Jews, nominal or active in their faith, in unpredictable and contradictory ways mirrored in the external world the spiritual processes driving my own interior life. Although I thought then that my own participation was individual and unique, I realized later it was part of a widespread ecumenical movement. I like to think now that in some way I was part of the efforts of John XXIII, who when he lived touched me as he did so many others, and the Second Vatican Council with its blast of fresh ecumenical air. Father M. Basil Pennington, commenting on this period and in this context, notes: "The Spirit is abroad now, among us as never before, enlivening us and calling us forth to ever fuller life."[10] This Spirit was, indeed, ecumenical.

Writing of Kabbalah and the Jewish experience in this connection, Perle Epstein muses: "On any plane going to and from India you see them, orange-robed, surrounded by worshipful American disciples—sixty per cent of whom, statistics tell us, are Jewish."[11] And only a little later, she addresses the other side of the coin:

> They [Kabbalah spiritual practices] are as valid a form of spiritual training as any from the Far East. In fact, many of them might talk more intimately to the Western

Jewish soul. I know a young woman who comfortably integrates her Indian meditation with her Hasidic ritual life. All kinds of interesting hybrids are possible.[12]

In that same period, spiritual seekers from the Christian community were encountering an identical spiritual "crisis." [They], Father Pennington wrote: "are flocking to the masters from the East to learn the methods of Zen and Yogic meditation, especially the Transcendental Meditation taught by Maharishi Mahesh Yogi."[13] Pennington, a Trappist monk, somewhat ruefully recounts a visit he made to a Ramakrishna temple in Chicago in the mid 1970s:

> Here I found twenty-four disciples gathered around a relatively young swami....His disciples were an impressive group, twenty-two to fifty-five years of age....All twenty-four were from Christian backgrounds. When I asked them what had drawn them to the temple, they invariably answered that they could find no one within their own Church who was willing to lead them into the deeper ways of the spirit where they could truly experience God.[14]

Looking back, I cannot escape the strange incongruity of this development on a personal level. The experience of transcendence derived from the teachings of the East was moving unsatisfied Christians and Jews into an alien religious tradition and at the same time moving people like myself, nonreligious Western individuals, back to the primal sources of Christianity. But as one moves back to those early sources it becomes less and less of a mystery. This stream of Christian thought and activity, originating with the earliest Christian teachings, generated and revealed the same interior stirrings of the presence of God that Eastern meditators understand as contact with Pure Consciousness—or the Vedic expression of this state, the Absolute.

I am struck today at the continuing strange resonances hindsight reveals in these events. The same confluence of Western and Eastern ideas and teachings that bubbled up and transformed those early Christians, and to which I was so clearly drawn, is repeating itself in contemporary life—and I found myself equally drawn to its modern expression. The great Christian mystical classics excited my soul. I felt a kinship with St. Teresa and her soul mate, John of the Cross. I found transcendence in Paul and Augustine, and the anonymous author of *The Cloud of Unknowing* became a beloved teacher. I found thrown into my path, as it were, voices from monasteries and convents through the inspired work of modern mystics like Merton. For almost three years I swam in the ocean of Christian mysticism and learned to treasure it. Then, also, I began to feel strangely close to the Catholic Church as I saw it as a shelterer, albeit a reluctant one, of this beautiful part of its body.

My interest and affection for these non-TM "disciplines" did not weaken my appreciation and love for my own meditative practice and its traditional teaching. But more than that, exposure to other systems strengthened my commitment to my practice. It is often said that a test for the validity of one's own spiritual path, *for that individual,* can be found in the appreciation and respect he or she develops for another's. This was my experience.

After a time, the intensity of my interest in other teachings began to diminish and I was able to appreciate them from a more equable level. It was a common experience among meditators to find expression for their growing spirituality through a renewed attraction to their personal traditions. But what had drawn me to Western mysticism, Jesus and charismatic Christians with such fervency, given the absence of these influences in my background? I could only now begin to fathom those forces, vastly more powerful and subtle than personal upbringing.

As I lost the emotional enthusiasm that had carried me to joyous heights, I was able to contemplate more objectively the uncanny, familiar quality arising from these other traditions. I wanted to understand this affinity for the various streams of spiritual awakening that had such deep roots in human history. Could it have its basis in a personal history which began far earlier than this present life?

Earlier, I discussed the ideas of karma and reincarnation and the insights they provided for understanding the events and transformations in my life. Now, again, these ideas are furnishing the clearest and most reasonable explanation of my developing emotional and intellectual state of mind. I sense that my deep attraction to this mystical aspect of Christianity, my neutral or antipathetic attitude toward its structure, and the reduction of my ardor toward it, has important psychological dimensions that require nontraditional explanations.

Nonetheless, I find it disconcerting when I am asked directly if I believe in these ideas. This kind of "knowledge" is not on the level of belief. I have a natural, intuitive conviction that the situations in my life which occur over and over again evoking the same response, negative or positive, exist because of action I instituted in the deep past, however distant that past and whatever the mechanics of its manifestation.

There is no real ideological component to this conviction, so I am free from the requirement to defend or promote it; this is not an insignificant blessing in itself. Through repeated contact with the healing power of transcendence, one's life is brought into line with natural law. Spontaneously, without effort, his discomfort with the experience of negativity diminishes and his attachment to the transitory nature of joy lessens. It is from this encounter the questions and doubts of "past life" influences and karmic bonds loosen and dissolve.

In this sense I understand my diminishing interest in Chris-

tianity. I am convinced I had some "unfinished business" or unre-
solved questions about my personal spiritual development which,
until decided, prohibited moving to other levels. These questions,
now finally settled, are no longer important or determining aspects
of my life. How all this affected my life before it was put to rest, in
what I know now to have been a spiritual catharsis, is no longer
relevant. Nor is it relevant or practical, were it even possible, to try
to examine the details of those past lives; it is enough to know that
the burdens of the past can be lifted through regular and continuous spiritual practice, and the freedom from these burdens will be
felt in the blessings of this lifetime.

These Western traditions that inspired my spiritual progress
and became a part of my life, are no longer an important part of it.
They were, one could almost say, static ripples of thought in a pond
of knowledge which began to deepen and broaden as my spiritual
life unfolded, and I became more firmly settled on my personal
path. But they remain beautiful milestones which I often revisit
and they are still able to move me to the emotional levels they did
when I first encountered them.

The Blessings II

As these new teachings became part of my consciousness, I began to cherish them not only for their intrinsic value, but also for their role as the underpinning of my increasingly positive self-image and changing personal relationships. Until one reaches a final level of fulfillment, that state that likely defies human expression, one never stops growing, and the understanding of this growth has an evolutionary value of its own.

But spiritual growth is an unpredictable phenomenon. There are areas of life that change so abruptly and with such impact that one is literally forced to take notice. Other changes, alternatively, are so subtle in form that no amount of introspection will reveal them. Some of these quiet changes can be illustrated by those physiological parameters such as lowered blood pressure measurements or favorable cholesterol readings, where improvements in these areas result from lower stress levels due to meditative practice. And there are other changes in consciousness reflective of growth that are so faint and tenuous they are easily overshadowed by the tumult of daily life. Fortunate indeed are they who can connect those insubstantial, almost hidden, changes to purposeful spiritual activity, and find in those connections the resources to sustain themselves in times when the raucous world erects seemingly impenetrable barriers to growth.

In my interior life, the psychological and emotional developments I had been undergoing were enormous, and the world was taking on a completely new reality. This was not simply a matter of different colored glasses altering one's perspective. In the case of different levels of consciousness, substance is affected as deeply as appearance. And in the case of householders such as myself, these metamorphoses must be made within the confines of a fixed social environment; I could not alter the fact of my multiple social roles: father, husband, breadwinner, etc., and retreat to the cloister or a Himalayan cave. Neither did I want to nor—more importantly—did I have to.

But there is a peculiar unevenness to spiritual growth. The resolution of negative and destructive psychological and emotional qualities in some areas of life are not equally resolved in other areas at the same time. Thus, those problems of socialization that I was so happily seeing diminish and disappear remained stubbornly resistant in my personal family. The anxiety and fears, the sense of insecurity, the problems of an assaulted ego, were largely gone or had become less important. But there remained in the relationships with our children much of the traditional parental difficulties bedeviling the lives of so many families. In some ways these were made worse because I now knew they were not necessary or fundamental to family life.

Florence and I completed our family in the late '60s and I was determined not to be a father like my own. I was consciously aware of the things I most sorely missed from him, and I wanted to be sure our children did not miss them from me. I was satisfied I was involving myself in their lives, participating in their activities, taking an interest in their needs and playing the typical traditional fatherly role in what was shaping up to be an apparently successful family. These were missing qualities in my relationship with my father, and I was convinced that that was the root of my problems with him and my own adolescent failures and unhappiness.

But what I failed to recognize then was that these were surface ideas—intellectual constructs which had no relationship to the deep, multifaceted emotional ties binding children to their parents. Going to Little League games has its importance, as do parent/teacher conferences, homework monitoring and, not least of course, love, support and affection. But the relationships between parents and children have their origins and fulfillment in a deep, hidden spiritual reservoir—recognized or not—which infuses all human relationships.

Trying to mediate these relationships without contacting that transcendent reservoir and drawing its influence into daily life means remaining on a one-dimensional surface of activity. Attempting to intellectually shift one's thinking from a negative to positive attitude, i.e., trying to will one's self into an emotionally blissful state, is like wagging a dog by the tail. Where that exercise is obviously an error, however, it is not that easy to see it as faulty thinking when other options are hidden. These insights were beginning to emerge on the basis of my experience with the spontaneous resolution of those identical problems of socialization that took place in my nonfamily social relationships.

Because this new way of looking at every aspect of my emotional life was so insistent, I began to reexamine the nature of my relationships with my children and to develop another understanding of my relationship with my late father. To be sure, the traditional family qualities have their value. Our family, in fact and in appearance was a solid one. Florence and I were sober and industrious. The children were successful in school, socially adjusted, preparing for and all finally achieving higher education. We had our share of adolescent problems, some more serious than others, but none of them violated the liberal humanistic values we believed in and tried to live by. I had believed that I escaped the sins of my father and provided for my family what he was unable to provide for his.

But I misunderstood my father's failure as a father and consequently my failures in turn. His sins were not because of his lack of participation or interest in my activities, nor did my participation and interest exculpate my own shortcomings. Rather, where we both fell short was in the inadvertent subverting of the needs and desires of our children, their unique instinctive and intuitive personal expression, to our own insecurities and fears. If my children wanted what I did not perceive as "practical," (read lucrative) or "prestigious," (read reflecting well on me) then I felt it was my duty to guide them into more successful ways. Despite our love for each other, this could not fail to create the same hostility and confusion that I so much wanted to avoid and which I detested in my own upbringing.

I say with a sense of contrition, my father was more innocent in this than was I. He, at least, genuinely believed he was doing his duty as a parent, whereas in the back of my mind I had the nagging sense that, in the apparent success of our family, I was replicating the same boyhood distorted and dysfunctional relationships I was so consciously determined to overcome. The Biblical writer of 20 Exodus warns of the jealousy of God: worshipping false gods results in visiting these sins from father to son to the fourth generation. The sins of pride, ambition, avarice, and envy were some of the false gods I was, through spiritual ignorance, mistakenly trying to placate through my children. I was failing to escape this cycle because of a poorly formed, only inchoate understanding of its existence.

But now the benefits accruing from my meditative practice began to force their way into these deeper parts of my life. Nevertheless, the fears and anxieties that earlier proved relatively vulnerable, were here resistant. I continued to feel and enjoy the freedom that characterized the other aspects of my social environment, but my apprehensions about my abilities as a father and my insecurities regarding the future of my children continued to plague me. The fact that I could not feel the same freedom from fear in this area that I did in that other social milieu disappointed and perplexed me, casting a discomforting shadow.

But this was a shadow, not an unmitigated darkness. That purifying force I was tapping every day was beginning to creep into our family relationships. I was picking away at, if only in tiny increments, that accumulation of ancient antagonisms poisoning our lives. And now I began to understand that our differences and conflicts were the result of a spiritual light yet too weak to find and enter those dark and distant crevices that were controlling our mutual destinies. What I had thought were fatherly efforts to protect and guide, were in reality a confused, inadequate, incomplete understanding of the bonds that united our shared lives. This recognition finally emerged as some of these deeply buried problems began to dissolve.

The first obvious indication that my parental role was assuming a new reality was the change in my relationship with my oldest son. This had been a time marked by growing painful difficulties between us and they were a source of sorrow, confusion and disappointment. These positive changes may have been predictable, since Ed introduced me to meditation several months after he himself started, and my initiation into TM was a way of entering and sharing an intimate area of his life. But I could not have consciously known that at the time and, moreover, neither of us could have anticipated the nature of these changes. This, despite the fact both of us were fortunate in quickly recognizing the value of our practice.

The "peak experiences" I described earlier that were so powerfully moving me and so significantly changing my life in other areas, finally began to work their magic here too. And in the same way, and for the same reason. My worries and fears for Ed's well-being, economic and social, became negligible as my own spiritual growth more and more negated these fears in myself. As a practical matter this could not have come at a more appropriate time. This was a period in my son's life that would burden the soul of any caring and practical father. Ed was just graduating from college with a degree in music, miniscule work experience, no money, in debt, a Salvation Army wardrobe, long hair, a beard and, it seemed to me, no future.

But strangely, this no longer mattered. Not only was I listening to his new "plans" uncritically, I found myself offering to abet them. Without going into the details of the next several years, had I not that growing inner sense of security we would have been completely alienated from each other. Ed violated every practical and common sense precept I lived by, but the fears and despair that should have been engendered in me by his lifestyle never materialized. Nor, tellingly enough, did the disasters materialize in his life that fed those unnecessary fears.

We lived in distant sections of the country, but we remained in close contact and I was aware of the changing cycles in his life. In those bumpy times when he needed assistance, I was pleased he found it possible to ask me and I was happy to be able to help him. The fact I was not fearful or concerned for him was an obvious boon for me, but it did as much, if not more, for him. He was free to pursue his own desires and find his own direction without the task of satisfying me or defending, fruitlessly, his every decision or act.

This realization of his freedom from my fears was the epiphany that led me to the understanding of how parental life can be fulfilled: children must be free to work out their own destiny, and the biggest obstacle to that freedom is parental fear—fear based too often on the personal desires and unsatisfied needs of the parents. This intuitive understanding, indicative of the growing influence of intuition as a concomitant of spiritual practice, was once again justified, as it was those other times when instinct and common sense rather than a clinical rationality determined my decisions. As Ed's life unfolds under his own direction, and in his own time, he is moving step by step toward greater satisfaction and increasing success. We did not completely work out our former problems; indeed, they continue to play a role in our relationship. But this new level of understanding is so overwhelming that the influence of that prior negativity is largely negligible and disappearing.

It is true Ed and I established a unique relationship based on our shared spiritual odyssey. But this did not mean the other children were not affected in the same way by my new level of functioning. Rather, this new understanding, more accurately, this new ability, to relate to them and function as a father, created a much more positive family structure. But unlike the situation with Ed, where we both recognized the transforming forces at work within us, the other members of the family were largely unaware of these hidden, and deep, changes. Several of them were initiated into TM during those first heady months but soon lost interest. Except for one daughter, my reports and descriptions of this spiritual metamorphoses had no significance for them.

My oldest daughter, Carol, was now out of college. She had a degree in education but was neither working as a teacher nor was she living at home nor near us. I was proud and impressed by her level of independence and competence, as was Florence, but I knew she was not sharing the details of her life with us; she understood correctly that neither Florence nor I would be happy with them. But we remained close and in contact. The fact there was no overt disapproval on our part and certainly no expressed parental demands that she live other than the way she chose, could not hide our implied or unexpressed anxieties. We shared these, I am sure, with all parents of children in that tumultuous transition period of the 1960s and 1970s.

Ed and Carol could not be more different in the way they lived. But the foreboding and tension they produced did not differentiate; I felt the same fears for each of them and with the same intensity. And in the same way these negative feelings softened and disappeared regarding Ed, they did so with Carol. The timing of my introduction to meditation was as appropriate for my relations with Carol as it was for my relations with him.

She quit her job in Boston and motored to Colorado, summering in the mountains. With no job and no apparent prospects, she talked of spending the winter "with friends in Denver." Typically, she did not tell us she applied to various school districts in the Southwest; a fact we did not learn until we got a phone call from a New Mexican school district wanting to interview her for a federally funded teaching position working with Native American children. The interview itself represented an almost thousand-mile journey through the Southwest in an old Volkswagen Beetle. This was an adventurous and testing period for her with few guarantees and many potential dangers.

No matter how clearly I understood on an intellectual level Carol's intelligence and appreciated her survival instincts, my traditional emotional response to her situation would have been one of worry, anticipating the worst, a constant concern nagging the back of my mind from telephone call to telephone call. But these worries and negative expectations did not materialize. My thoughts of her were episodic, occasioned when we would have news for her, or when she would call with news of events in her life. As she established herself in her new location, settling into her job, finding suitable housing and adapting to a completely new social environment, she achieved an independence and individual identity. Like her brother, she successfully expressed in the living of her life the intrinsic goal of all parenting: the production of a complete, separate individual capable of a self-determining and successful existence.

These insights into "enlightened" parenting emerged spontaneously in my awareness, not because of some clever reasoning. I was able to realize them because I was living without the gross apprehensions that would have otherwise distorted my understanding. I remember the many occasions I had told my mother about one or another undertaking I was considering. Invariably she would express her fears. When I implored her not to worry about me she would reply, "I worry about you because I love you so much." This thinking was previously as much a part of my emotional temperament as it was my mother's. Now, for the most part, the worry was gone and the love, for the first time, was able to reach full flower.

Carol and Ed, as the two oldest, were the first to challenge this level of emotional stability and the understanding it engendered. I know with absolute certainty that had I not been able to accept their lifestyles, and the direction in which they were being moved by them, our lives would have been strained and conflicted with all the joys of accomplishments, theirs and mine, polluted by anger and bitterness. The failure of my parents and me to resolve these similar questions ultimately soured much of our lives together, and all the signs of repeating this failure were there. That gift of equanimity stemming from my daily meditation practice was the saving factor in this new and productive association, and it was now the ever-present mediator in all my relationships, overshadowing, if not completely eliminating, those former worries.

Our relationship with our other children had not reached the same potential for disaster because they were younger and not yet ready to entirely sever their parental moorings. In addition, they saw how their older siblings were faring and saw no reason they would not be able to do the same. But I learned I could not confer on them the lessons and understanding now informing my life. Indeed, for most of them my meditation was a parental oddity with little or no impact on their lives. They were so focused on their own needs, fighting their own insecurities and fears, they could not sense these subtle, hidden changes in me.

In addition, freedom from the parental fears that distort normal family interaction does not eliminate the need for guidance, responsibility and discipline. The children still at home pushed in vain for motorcycles, early driving lessons, greater television privileges and lower demands for academic achievement.

But more than that, I do not believe there are relationships with stronger and deeper roots than those of family ties, especially in the relationship of parents and children. For this reason, no matter how well resolved emotional problems prove to be in other areas, these special bindings resist solution to the last. And then, when the influences of the past would finally ease, long ingrained mechanical habits of response would take over. Consequently, although I was enjoying a more positive level of our interaction, from their perspective, the same stubbornness, nonsupport and lack of understanding they always felt from me continued.

But from my side it would not be the same. Although I could not release them from the emotional problems created by their own situation in life, I could at least understand them and not feed into them and make them worse. This understanding helped me to step back from serious confrontations, to accept fault—which is not easily done even when deserved—and permitting activities that would have met refusal in the past.

This had some interesting and ironic consequences and the following story is illustrative of this new level of family communication. Our daughter, Patrice, decided to pursue her college Junior year in Iceland. Although we had some misgivings and questioned this decision, her decision was not unreasonable given her academic interests, and she was able to defend it on those grounds. After we agreed, we gave her what support we could and helped her prepare for her trip. She spent a productive year; first in Iceland and then some unstructured, and unsupervised, time in England and Ireland.

This was an important transition time in her life as she was entering independent adulthood. Some years later, at a time of self-evaluation, she pointed to this period as an example of our parental failure. She complained that when she proposed her trip to Iceland we made no effort to stop her, in fact, she indicated, she really did not want to go to Iceland. It seemed to her that by not opposing her trip we did not care whether she went or not and failed to provide the emotional support she needed for her to change her mind. I need not point out that had we refused to allow her to go— she required parental approval—she would have pointed to that refusal as an example of incorrect and unsupportive parenting. In this case, she would have complained, about how we always resisted her plans.

The perennial conundrum of families with children is the question of "fairness." Blessed, and few in number, are those brothers or sisters who do not feel resentment of the parent who responds to the neediest sibling. That this is an ancient problem, and one equally problematic for a heavenly as well as an earthly father, is made clear by Luke's recounting of Jesus' parable of the prodigal son. When the sinful and wastrel son returns after squandering his inheritance, the father prepares a great feast to welcome his return. The good son scolds his father, complaining the father never prepared such a feast for him, although he was steadfast all these years. And the father replied: "My son, you are with me always and all I have is yours. But it was only right we should celebrate and rejoice, because your brother here was dead and had come to life; he was lost and is found."

But the question of suffering and its cessation in the family environment, I began to realize, were not issues that resulted from poor or sound juvenile or parental judgments. Rather, these matters have deep spiritual significance. The fact that one child or another, or one person or another, appears to play a larger role in illuminating and resolving these questions does not lessen the importance of the others. In this connection, the two children whose lives were destined to challenge the limits of our emotional resources were now preparing to enter that stage. My daughter, Maria, was ending a difficult transition to adulthood with a life-threatening disease, and my youngest son, Steven, was on the threshold of a tumultuous and destructive adolescence.

For my part, without the support of a spiritual practice that allowed me to place those experiences into a manageable perspective, the difficulties we were preparing to face could well have proved devastating. I understood then on an intuitive level, what I can now comfortably and confidently express, that the suffering I was sharing with my children and my wife, and which appeared to have been caused by their suffering, was in reality due to my own actions in the past, just as their suffering was due to their past actions.

Some years later, I came across a little book containing early lectures and question/answer sessions by Maharishi. One of these questions speaks directly to this matter. A listener asks:

Maharishi, What about the suffering of a child?

Maharishi replies:

> His own doing. Suffering means the result of some wrong doing in the past, that is all, whether the child suffers or the old man suffers. The child is suffering, and due to the

suffering of the child, mother suffers and father suffers. Now the father and mother are suffering not due to the suffering of the child, but due to their own actions of the past. Suffering is one's own repayment of deeds. The theory of Karma, the theory of action is very clear, no ambiguity, no complications there. As you sow so you shall reap. Meditation is an action which takes a man out of the influences of relativity. Come out of the experience, out of the binding influence of action, right into the eternal freedom of life. That is why we have a message of meditation. It does away with all the complexities of Karma and everything.[1]

This understanding of suffering acts as a powerful liberating force in the life of the individual who can accept it. But this acceptance is not a function of intellect; rather, it is an existential experience that occurs in the unfolding of life itself. One cannot escape past action, karma, but one can mitigate and end its influence with present action, also karma, and this human ability represents the fulfillment of Western philosophy's concept of free will and Buddha's four Noble Truths.

As Maria's struggle with Hodgkin's disease progressed, an apparent emotional "distancing" from the seriousness of her condition led to some confused reactions. She took full control of her treatment. Although she kept us informed of every step, it was clear we had little input into these decisions. From our side, we supported her in every way and never felt the need to question or doubt her judgment. Florence and I both believed she was better able to decide the course of treatment herself. Events proved her course was the correct one. If we did involve ourselves in these questions, speaking to doctors and searching for medical advice, we could not have brought about a better outcome, and likely we would have caused confusion and greater stress. At a later date, however, Maria, like her sister before her, complained about our detachment and lack of concern. In our culture it seems, if there is no beating of the breast and the tearing of clothing, grief, sympathy and worry do not exist.

At the very time of Maria's trial a singular event occurred that illustrates the point made by Maharishi on suffering and illustrates as well the difficulty of isolating that point from the experience of relative life. I entered a state of despair so deep I thought I was losing my mind. Florence saw glimpses of this condition but otherwise I faced it alone. A dark knot of anguish materialized in the pit of my stomach that was so palpable I felt it as a physical object. Its presence was a continuous sense of doom, whether in the fitful sleep I was able to find, or during daily activity. It was impossible to meditate. When I closed my eyes to begin my practice it seemed every cell of my body would bring its attention to that point of distress and I found myself pounding the floor to try to relieve the pain. This must be, I thought then, the overwhelming despair that drives people to suicide.

This condition lasted, I estimate now, approximately seven days and it coincided with Maria's exploratory surgery and her confinement. Although I am not perfectly sure what brought any of this on, I offer with hesitation the following reflection, more out of a sense it should be told than to assert a definite analysis. I remember thinking at that time, regarding the anxiety Maria would be feeling about her condition, that if I could not help her otherwise, perhaps I could assume some of that anxiety. I understood on some level or another—how, I cannot say—that it may be possible to redirect that anxiety and fear through me. I remember asking that that redirection take place. Whatever the cause of that event, its onset was sudden. Less clear was the cause of its lifting, although it was equally sudden.

Toward the end of this time, I received a call from Maharishi International University (MIU), recruiting people to a large meditation course in Fairfield, Iowa. The idea of attending in that emotional state was impossible. But during the conversation I felt the sense of dread begin to lift. It was less a lifting than a dissolving in that afflicted area—the sense of a material mass becoming smaller until it was gone. That evening I experienced my first normal meditation since the ordeal began and that meditation marked the end of it.

This experience, like many that came before, had that isolated purity about it I have now come to associate with karmic release. The striking thing about these events is their association with external conditions sometimes and their separation from them at other times. Thus, although their onset and their end can be marked by incidents in the environment, they do not have to be. And in this case, as in others, the experience came to an end before the condition that it was seemingly associated with ended. Moreover, and to me most significantly, it left no residue of emotion, no feeling about it. It came, it ran its course and it was gone. Even its memory conjures up no pain.

The value and validity of this new level of functioning, and the insights it provided, were proven over and over again as our son Steven moved into his teen years and beyond. His high school years were an horrendously stressful time for him and us. His life was focused on drugs, The Grateful Dead rock group, and vehicles. In those early years, his lifestyle was one we could not countenance and we did not know even then the extent of his abuse. He barely graduated from high school, and to this day we dispute who had greater responsibility for this achievement, he or we.

But no matter how much the provocation, we never lost meaningful contact. Time after time in that period, he would drive me to the edge of an emotional precipice, only for the episode to end at that point, enabling us to start anew. The great blessing of that growing ability within me to end a negative and hostile situation without recrimination, saved—and indeed nourished—what could have been a totally destructive relationship. Free from those old parental needs and drives, I was able to see in him that stable and positive core his many supportive friends and employers were able to see. On that basis, his considerable innate merit, and my willingness to search for it, established a flourishing ideal relationship we both treasure.

I feel that same sense of satisfaction and contentment unmixed with any disappointment for David and James, my other children. In both cases, they overcame the difficulties of adolescence and young adulthood while laying the intellectual and emotional foundation for successful lives. Like the others, they pushed against and expanded the disciplinary limits we imposed, but as they bent and broke ours they erected their own positive standards. They have all passed the point where they need parenting and I have no desire to continue it. I take no credit for this; their independence and maturity, of which they are rightfully proud, is their own responsibility and achievement.

Biological family ties, with its supporting science of genetics, provide an element of rationality to the concept of children and parents coming together to fulfill common needs arising out of possible past lives. This idea may seem to have less objective validity in Western marriages where free choice and divorce almost run hand in hand. But when the spiritual light of transcendental understanding is thrown on these unions they, too, are seen as the coming together of separate souls for their own individual reasons.

Changes in my married life, and my relationship with my wife due to my spiritual practice, were far less clear than they were with my children or my parents and siblings. But this new light revealed dimensions in our union which I could never have otherwise realized. My marriage, I would have said, was a good and solid one with few marital problems, most of which came and went, resolving themselves simply through the passage of time.

Perversely, it was my spiritual practice, which Florence tried to enter and share despite her lack of desire or interest, that caused more confusion and unhappiness than we previously experienced. It is a strange irony that this practice, which represented the first real threat to this successful and productive shared life, also revealed the nature of that unity and Florence's unique and indispensable contribution to its success and maintenance. The oftentimes self-centered demands and confusion engendered by my spiritual activities could not overwhelm the evenness of her temperament, her flexibility and, above all, her selflessness. I have not always understood or appreciated this.

My marriage to Florence, now approaching its 50th year, violated all the traditional hallmarks for success. We came from completely different backgrounds, I from a lower middle-class Jewish family, Florence from a working-class farming background. My grandparents came from areas in Ukrainian and Lithuanian Russia. I was born and raised in New York City. Florence was born on a farm in Ossining, N.Y., from parents who came from a southern Italian rural area. Despite these differences, which were greater in other ways not easily detailed here, I was immediately drawn to her when we met. Within a year we were married, I at age twenty-eight and she at twenty-five.

For me, no better decision could have been made, although Florence will have to speak for herself on this matter. Within the structure of this marriage, she created an environment of acceptance and support that permitted my life to unfold in its own way, step by step, by trial and error and trial again. Without skills or formal education, I managed only an incremental improvement in our living standards, and for most of our lives together we were able to do little more than satisfy our basic needs. I was well aware of my inadequacies as a provider, but never once did she complain or allow me to feel diminished because of it.

There are many ways to look at a relationship such as this and one's role in it. But here, as in any other significant lifetime association, no greater clarity can be brought to its evaluation than a spiritual perspective: that the purpose of a relationship is to provide its participants the structure, environment and challenge to promote holistic growth. Too often, alas, knowledge of that purpose is revealed only when it is achieved. But it is a splendid achievement, indeed, for in that evaluation and accomplishment the remnants of whatever ill-will was created by the struggles and hostility of past years are dissolved. This is a relationship lived in freedom and love.

Chapter Nine
Integration

1 987 was a personal watershed year. My mother passed away at age ninety-three, after a short illness. While laying her to rest in accordance with her wishes, I remember a feeling of satisfaction that we had no unfinished business that would have required more time. I am not sure she understood, as clearly as I felt I did, the purpose of our lives together, but she indicated in those final few years that she thought of me with love and respect and as a complete person. I, in turn, tried to convey to her my recognition of her life as one of struggle and devotion. She was pleased when I expressed these thoughts. Certainly, the old hostilities and misunderstandings were long gone.

Also in that year, my youngest son became twenty-one, so all my children were adults; in tradition, in law and in fact. To be sure, there were situations that required the usual parental functions, but they were in large part habitual and formal. When intervention in their lives met with resistance, as it often did, I was able to retreat without a sense of rejection. In fact, I believe their strong tendency toward independence was more appreciated by me, than my willingness to stop parenting was appreciated by them.

But as important as these milestones were, they were eclipsed by a personal circumstance that had a greater impact on my life. I reached formal retirement age, sixty-five, at which point I had moved onto a new platform of security, although I was not planning on retiring. Ironically, when I finally reached that juncture, one that I so longingly anticipated for years, I was hesitant to enter it. I enjoyed excellent working conditions in a somewhat stress-free position. My sixty-fifth birthday came and went, and for a number of compelling reasons I planned to continue to work.

Overnight this situation changed. My company was the victim of an hostile takeover. The new management moved my position to a distant location, and new supervision made it clear that the respect and privilege I earned over the years, the intangible values of employment, were not part of the package acquired by them with the office equipment and furniture. Retirement, therefore, turned out to be the best option after all, even though it was a decision not largely my own. I realize now I spent the following two years as preparation for the next significant phase of my life, one that would have a markedly transforming influence.

The actual fact of retirement became a time of assessment. For the first time in almost fifty years I did not have to make a living. For most of that time, moreover, I had been responsible for the material well-being of a large family. Often in those times I suffered the pangs of despair and fear over my inability to properly discharge this responsibility. Now those fears were largely gone. My most positive fantasies then were the ones in which I was finally, successfully released from these obligations. And now, paradoxically, when those dreams were realized, I could not feel that rush of exhilaration one would expect from a normally exciting state of affairs.

Retiring was an event that imposed on my awareness a different satisfaction. Rather than great joy or excitement, I felt a sense of peace, freedom, equanimity. I knew this was a result of my meditative practice, of course, for over the years these emotions had become a recognized pattern in my life. But at this point another quality crept into my consciousness; I began to understand more clearly how the support of natural law manifests in the affairs of individuals and how easily these manifestations can be hidden and ignored. There are those who speak of these forces as the work of "spirit guides" or "going with the flow." But I had first heard of the idea as "the support of nature," and now it became an enlivening force as I realized its effect.

It was more than a dozen years since I was initiated into the Transcendental Meditation program, and for about the last six of these years I had been practicing advanced forms of this technique. It is easy enough now to conclude these were the most productive years of my life, but it is only on the basis of hindsight that this conclusion can be reached. During that period I dealt with each event as it occurred, not understanding its connections or purposes. Indeed, there was little thought of purpose or meaning beyond the event itself. Although glimpses and intuitive impulses would surface and be noted, it was difficult, if not impossible, to appreciate the ever-rising quality of well-being entering my life amid the ever-changing tumult of the typical modern society.

This realization first surfaced on a mostly mundane level, albeit an important one, when we examined our financial status at retirement. We initially thought most of our retirement income would come from my Social Security benefits and Florence's wages. We found, however, that the decisions we made the previous ten years, in connection with various shared investment plans developed by my company, combined with the thrifty lifestyle which we ordinarily lived, would enable us to maintain the identical standard of living that we had during our latest and best earning period.

None of these decisions were made out of an astute understanding of investment practices. We were not burdened with the desire or need to accumulate large amounts of money so we followed a naturally cautious financial approach. An approach, arising no doubt, from our Great Depression-born respect for money and our difficulty in acquiring it. Several years later, when

Florence retired, we were in a situation I had never before thought possible: we could live the way we always had without working.

In my mind, this financial security and the freedom it accorded was a positive result of my spiritual practice. The past dozen or so years of my life were not so different than the previous dozen in their external circumstances. They all involved a struggle to make a living with falling and rising fortunes in the work place. Unemployment and its consequences were part of both segments. Family problems, economic worries, successes mixed with failures, all represented the constant giving and taking away, the acquiring and losing, that marks the nature of normal life. The total difference, in all their aspects, however, between these two times was that in the latter period I was meditating and in the former I was not. I saw this as the difference between living in light and living in darkness.

Other reasons could have been given for this financial and emotional security. All are obvious and practical. During this period we paid off our mortgage, the economy changed for us, our children were leaving the house, Florence went to work, and, finally, I acquired more personal maturity. But I knew in the deepest level of my being that that last period of years was blessed by my daily contact with the dynamic quietness of the creating forces of the universe. No aspect of my life was untouched by this contact. But I also knew it is impossible to convey to others that personal, economic and emotional circumstances, all of them, are a function of one's internal resources; this awareness can only be a shared experience.

A growing realization of the influence of transcendental consciousness in my life then began to develop. More and more my surface existence reflected a growing internal silence. Since I was out of the economic struggle I had faced during the previous fifty years, this could be seen as a naturally occurring phenomenon reflecting a general lessening of stress. But that could not explain attitudinal changes unrelated to that economic need. Even episodes of negativity in social and family life were thought of as having positive consequences, in the sense they were releases of past negative incidents that I would no longer have to face. I was seeing everything in terms of spiritual growth, but I did not realize how much I internalized this Pollyannaish state of mind until my wife actually called me a "Pollyanna," in pique at my generally upbeat manner.

In Connecticut, where I live, the State University system offers tuition-free schooling for senior citizens. This fact brought to the surface of my mind long gestating thoughts of acquiring a formal education. Over the years I acquired more than enough academic knowledge to satisfy both commercial and social needs, but I was always troubled by its lack of structure and by the huge gaps in my education. Getting a college degree now became fixed in my mind as a personal goal. This goal, combined with the knowledge that for the first time in my life I did not have to work, determined my course for the immediate future.

I made the decision to attend the local university for two reasons: the first, and the most conscious one, was to get the education I long wanted; but the second reason, which I could not then have known, revealed the significance and the power of unfolding spirituality in the life of an individual. Education was the most meaningful pursuit I could have then followed to carry my spiritual evolution forward. It was the vehicle to bring into consciousness that vast array of practical, albeit immaterial, benefits which derive from spiritual practice, rewards which play their vital role unrecognized and hidden, yet stand revealed when given the opportunity.

This decision to go to school was also the beginning of the integration of what were then well-defined but separate qualities in my experience. On the surface I continued the ordinary activities that were part of normal daily life. Beneath this level, however, were the continual ethereal impulses, often unexpressed even in my own consciousness, that kept me aware of and bound to an ever-deepening center. My regular daily meditative exercises were done in private. And my frequent weekend and longer meditation "retreats" were always in a protected environment designed purposely to maximize the transcendental experience. Now I began to recognize new dimensions of the expression of what Maharishi calls "creative intelligence" in the mechanics of daily circumstances.

I was sixty-seven years old, in March, 1989, when I entered the registration office of Western Connecticut State University (WCSU) in Danbury. I removed the last obstacle to my entrance to college when I completed my examination for a General Education Diploma (GED). The registration clerk who shepherded my application for enrollment as a matriculated student made me feel I was a priority candidate by the way she patiently dealt with my special needs. The entire process from the time of my initial decision and inquiries, through GED preparation and examination, through registration and acceptance as a student, took no more than three months.

Before I knew it, I was swept into an environment that shortly became the center of a new world of interest for the next six years, first as an undergraduate and then as a graduate student. I started receiving notices for placement tests, summer courses and orientation seminars. I was required to arrange a schedule for fall classes. Since I had the time and the university was close by, I established my own orientation procedures. In a short time all of my organizational and mechanical needs were met, and I was reasonably familiar with the location of support facilities, making personal contact with faculty advisors and administration personnel.

That summer I attended my first college course. This "Introduction to Political Science" class was an ideal choice for my first exposure to the academic side of college. It helped ease my way into this new sphere of organized study, tests, and papers. The subject matter was familiar to me, and since I had spent many years aware of and interested in domestic and international events, I did not have to struggle with the content. In addition, summer classes attract a disproportionate number of nontraditional students—those over twenty-five years of age—and upperclassmen. Although I was then the oldest person in the classroom, and remained so virtually throughout my college years, I felt at home.

That summer class experience was a useful introduction to what I would encounter later. But nothing could have prepared me for that first day on campus as an incoming freshman. My first class, "Writing About Literature," consisted of teen-age students not much further from their sixteenth year than I was from my sixty-fifth. To make it even more bizarre, the instructor was a graduate student only a few years older than most of the other freshmen. With the exception of a more mature professorial staff, that demographic pattern held for most of the next four years.

Again, the sense of being at ease in unfamiliar surroundings served to connect me with my spiritual practice. When I first encountered this experience it was with the joy of realizing the positive effects of my meditation. And over time that experience has become deeper and clearer. I felt connected to an internal, infinite center that defined me as a person and when I sat down in that undergraduate classroom, circular in form, I faced these students as simply another student.

An intangible sense of great security emerged as I sat there and realized our surface differences were meaningless. Because of my lack of self-consciousness, it was only a short time until I was accepted as part of the student body, and before the semester ended we entered a pleasant and mutually beneficial academic experience.

People normally think of their daily activity and affairs in terms of correct or incorrect decisions or good or bad luck. But I realized I no longer thought on that level when I began to see the effortless character of the materialization of this desire to go to school. This cognition has no scientific validity, but it is hardly unique. It has been noted by self-development and Jungian psychologists, noted as well as a concomitant of spiritual practice in the *Bhagavad-Gita,* and noted no less by fellow meditators. Problems no sooner arose than they were solved. When I asked for help with one administrative question or another, the response was invariably positive and patient. This comes to mind because I remember the constant complaints by other students about the testiness of university aides. My student friends thought, reasonably, I was treated differently because of my years.

There were so many "meaningful coincidences" where things came together to support my needs with no possible reference to this factor that each new incident only served to reinforce my convictions. One illustration will make that point. I needed an English class to satisfy my freshman second semester schedule. The system then was lower classes registered later so it was possible for freshmen to miss out on core classes and be forced to rearrange their schedule over and over. Since I had to wait for upperclassmen to make their selections, there was a good chance I would miss out on this core class. I was not surprised then, when I applied for it that the student aide said she thought it was filled, but to make sure she casually looked through the file box and found one card left that was somehow stuck to the back of the plastic box. "Gosh," she said, "are you lucky, I never saw that card before."

All the rewards from meditation that played their previous transforming role in my personal and social life now began to influence my behavior as a student. The different circumstances provided an opportunity for them to be appreciated anew. The wide disparity in the ages of the other students and me represented an enormous test. It would be ordinary and normal were I a teacher, a mentor, or a counselor. But as a fellow student it was an "odd" relationship. I felt different, perhaps like disabled students may feel knowing special accommodations must be provided for them, and finding themselves the center of unwanted attention because of it. I embraced the academic part of student life easily enough, and that became a natural bridge to enter more meaningful and productive associations with the other students. But our common academic needs were the least of the factors that determined our interactions. And now, those constructive social abilities engendered by meditation found a new outlet for expression. In a short time I lost any inhibiting sense of my age. I was open to new experience with an easy attitude the younger students appreciated. I was always included in the small study groups that were organized and, later, in upper classes, the older and more serious students sought me out to center or lead these groups. I earlier mentioned this "feeling at home" phenomenon in connection with an employment experience; it continues to delight me.

Student language and behavior was often gross, but I never entered their life on that level. I expected and received respect due to my mature status, yet at the same time we were able to establish the affectionate bonds that characterizes shared institutional experience. This situation was perfect for the flowering of those life-supporting attributes signifying universal spirituality.

I worked hard and strove for good grades, the only academic measure of success, if not the best one. But if there was any sense of competition in this it was with myself; never did I feel I wanted to hold back knowledge from another student. Rather, it was with a real sense of friendliness and compassion that I shared my efforts and abilities. I recall spending hours working with and mastering the "mysteries" of college level algebra. And I felt satisfaction later when I was able to help bring others to passing levels, and I felt this without any sense that I was being exploited or used because of students who would not, or could not, exert the same effort.

I realized the "spiritual" quality of this attitude when another "mature" student friend, equally hard working and successful, remarked how tired he was of helping these "kids" who did not want to work and only wanted to just get by. He was right, of course, as so many of them did fit that category. But that did not matter to me. I had this to give and I wanted to offer it for my own reasons and needs. The recipient's attitude was his problem. Indeed, often there would be no thanks or any indication of appreciation. But when we would encounter each other at another time my attitude would be the same if he were the greatest or least thankful student. Moreover, this was not as unfair as it seemed; the hard working and more interested person usually continued to receive the most attention. In addition, although this may not seem so at first glance, it is also a very productive state of mind. When one is little concerned or affected by the imagined or real negative consequences of a potentially hostile interaction, the energy saved and the stress avoided is of great value.

I know exactly how altruistic and unworldly this sounds. Nevertheless, these qualities were not new or recognized as new. They stemmed from the equanimity and selflessness, the lack of self-consciousness and the presence of personal security that my spiritual practice generated and which marked previous situations. This new environment simply allowed them to be expressed in a different way. I can describe this personal state of mind candidly, without a sense of immodesty, because I take no personal credit for these character traits. I had always known they represented a higher level of ethical and moral functioning. Yet when I had made an effort to incorporate them in my life it was with great strain, with intermittent results, and with ambiguous feelings about their value. My first priority had always been self-interest, which I thought of as contradictory to a generous spirit. However, I finally came to realize it is the spontaneous rise of this generous spirit that provides the highest personal good.

This level of behavior and psychological state, I hasten to add, was mixed with the frustrations, difficulties and confusion all students faced. When periods of negativity materialized I responded accordingly, but always with a heightened sense of this being an unworthy, and an unnecessary response. These times were typically short lived and, consistent with my now accustomed reaction to negativity, they left without a trace. I still do not weary of remarking on the spontaneous appearance and growth of these ethereal abilities following TM initiation and my exposure to the reality of transcendence. I continue to wonder at it all.

This dimension of school experience gave new meaning and expression to the emotional content of those early esoteric spiritual teachings. The qualities of love, affection and helpfulness that those teachings represented, I now came to appreciate as an unfolding of a spiritual path of its own. This productive and totally enjoyable relationship with the student body and faculty uplifted my entire school life.

But there is another area to a university experience that plays an equal role in spiritual development: the growth of greater cognitive and intellectual abilities that had been for so many years observed in meditators and associated with spiritual practice. This growth can be seen no more clearly than in academic life. I had always been aware of the research indicating improved mental functioning in people on a regular spiritual program. However, the psychological and emotional quality-of-life benefits were so overwhelming that I tended to regard those cognitive improvements as a side effect of my practice. The ability to increase one's overall intellectual power is inarguably a great talent; but few would argue that living a life without anger, fear, envy, frustration or hostility is also no small thing. And now, in this academic setting, the intellectual benefits from meditation I had previously relegated to a fringe area were given full rein; mind and heart had become integrated.

This was not as easily seen in my core requirement classes, many of which I was able to "CLEP" out of through approved examinations. This "College Level Examination Program" was available for nontraditional students entering as freshman. It was in my upper level classes, however, especially in Philosophy, and English, that I realized dimensions of understanding which had clearly surfaced on the basis of my meditation experience. By this time, I had been meditating for more than fifteen years and daily contact with the reality of transcendence had become as familiar as breathing, and just as automatic.

I now became aware of how this contact, combined with the knowledge necessary to understand and appreciate it, determined the way I looked at all knowledge, and indeed the world. Maharishi's insistence that the ability to transcend is a universal human facility, not limited to a specific religion or philosophy, encouraged the exploration of non-Vedic, or "universal" approaches to understanding the phenomenon. His training as a physicist, perhaps, allowed him early to recognize the identity between the "Pure Consciousness" of the Vedas and the "Unified Field" of Western physical science. It is only in the past several decades that Western scientists and writers had begun to make this same connection.

In general, my identification with the esoteric writings and ideas of Eastern and Western mysticism had provided the most satisfying and inspiring impact on my spiritual life. Vedic masters, Western hagiography, modern Theosophy and New Age revelation were long-term companions in this journey. I had been exposed to the relationship between these ideas and modern physics through various Western scientific and philosophical writers, but I had never been inspired by the exploration of the mechanics of subatomic particle "reincarnation" as I was by the working out of my own past life concerns. My new intellectual environment, however, began to stimulate an interest in these connections as my expanding world view encompassed and unified what were no longer disparate teachings.

I found a spiritual connection with the lives and work of our Western scientific geniuses, as I learned how the discoverers reacted in their first encounter with this new world. According to quantum physics, the essence of the physical world is not knowable. Its basic subatomic components are neither particles nor nonparticles, but, incredibly both, exhibiting the nature of either a particle or a wave depending on what and where the observer directs his or her attention. In a real sense, these people had come to the end of the physical world. So far as most theoretical physicists were concerned, Erwin Schrodinger's development of wave function theory, which describes this paradox, is said to be the most complete description of physical reality possible.[1] Reality on this level is a field of all possibilities; anything can emerge and all we can really know is the *probability* of the status of an event. This system in its quiescent, undisturbed state exhibits an infinite number of possibilities. But as soon as a detection device, ultimately a human consciousness, tries to examine it, one possibility of that limitless number *particularizes*, or manifests, and the wave function collapses as a specific world emerges. There is no objective universe, no world apart from the perception of an observer. In a very real sense, the world is created by the observer. Physicist Henry Stapp writes:

> If the attitude of quantum mechanics is correct, in the strong sense that a description of the substructure underlying experience more complete than the one it provides

is not possible [sic] then there is no substantive physical world, in the usual sense of this term. The conclusion here is not the weak conclusion that there may not be a substantive physical world but rather that there definitely is not a substantive physical world.[2]

All new world-changing ideas are threatening, as I clearly remembered from my early meditation days, and quantum physics is no exception. Max Planck, its discoverer, was so deeply disturbed by his findings he published his paper with the hope other physicists would disprove it.[3] Albert Einstein, for one, resisted for his entire life the conclusion forced by this discovery—that rational thought cannot give a complete understanding of the world. Although incorporating Planck's quantum theory in his work, he could not accept "that God plays dice with the world." In the end, despite the objections of Einstein and others, "...for the first time, scientists attempting to formulate a consistent physics were forced by their own findings to acknowledge that a complete understanding of reality lies beyond the capabilities of rational thought."[4] Although this is not the first time scientists and others regretted the consequences of their work, it is always a poignant moment when one finds one's work the cause of despair. Werner Heisenberg wrote in this context:

> I remember discussions with Bohr [in 1927] which went through many hours till very late at night and ended almost in despair; and when at the end of the discussion I went alone for a walk in the neighboring park I repeated to myself again and again the question: Can nature possibly be as absurd as it seemed to us in these atomic experiments.[5]

What these scientists accomplished, in fact, was the virtual destruction of their 300-year-old Newtonian universe. The Vedic concept of the absolute underlying field of all possibilities was forced on them by their own brilliant work. The only thing left for them was to create an organizing system of thought structuring this new knowledge. Modern scientists are doing that today by integrating the subjectively revealed wisdom of the East with the objective genius of the West.

I had been absorbing these ideas through some kind of mental osmosis for many years, but I had no idea how much a part of my thinking they had become until they emerged full blown in my school work. My academic pursuits became a spiritual exercise as I began to see this level of reality in the subjects I was studying. Surely I was not the first to glimpse the possible, or probable, influence of Eastern thought on Plato, who with Socrates, his teacher, laid the basis for Western philosophical thinking; but these correlations emerged in my mind as I studied their work, and I recognized the internal stirrings that had become familiar to me as a "spiritual experience."

I use Plato as an example for a personal reason: all my life I had heard references to him but I was ignorant of everything beyond the most elementary knowledge of Greek philosophy. As I now entered into his world and his mind, I found familiar territory illuminating not only my intellect but also my heart. More than once, I was reminded of Socrates' attempt to convince Menon that nothing is learned, all was known from past lives and these recollected impressions take form in the present.[6] Most of my subjects were appreciated on this level; because I was acutely aware of the transcendent reality underpinning all knowledge, and my experiential consciousness of it, I was able to see dimensions in these subjects often otherwise overlooked. One can imagine the contribution that can be made to a class on this basis, a contribution, I am gratified to say, that was appreciated by most students and professors.

My five undergraduate years were as successful as they were exhilarating. I enjoyed the esteem and affection I received and the satisfaction I felt when I could instruct and tutor, and when I was asked on occasion to participate in class instruction. When some members of the faculty encouraged me to take postgraduate studies and teach freshman writing as a Graduate Assistant, I seized on that idea with enthusiasm. I remember thinking, I would not want to be anywhere else but here.

However, this overwhelming support from all sides had another consequence; it masked the nascent stirrings of opposing feelings. My personal interest and keenness for the discipline and structure of academic life began to fade just as family and friends eagerly encouraged me to pursue new academic goals. I found it increasingly difficult to continue at my former spirited level. What had before been a joy to do was now becoming a chore.

I had gotten myself into this conflicting situation through a failure to recognize I had stopped listening to my interior guide. The encouragement and to a large extent the admiration, which included local newspaper coverage making me out to be something of a role model, went to my head. Step by step I went deeper into this program until I understood I was not acting in accordance with my needs or interests, and these negative consequences were affecting not only me but also my immediate environment.

With this realization came the decision to resign from the graduate program. The decision itself was immediately vindicated by the change in my outlook and emotional state; it was as if I were catapulted past the last rock barrier of a turbulent rapids into the calmly flowing river.

This represented the virtual end of my college days, and I began to sense a more far-reaching completion was at hand. I took a semester leave, then went back for another graduate course, but I realized it was more out of habit than desire. At this point, I no longer have any formal ties to the University, and for all practical purposes my householder responsibilities have come to an end. In what direction my life will now move I do not know. But, as the idea of writing this spiritual odyssey begins to stir in my mind, I know it is the first step into new beginnings. I look forward to the future with confidence and anticipation.

Chapter Nine
Epilogue

I find myself reluctant to leave this book. In a way, this feeling echoes my initial reluctance to writing it. I overcame that hesitancy to share with an ever-growing spiritual community my own personal awakening and transformation, as I more and more realized the commonality of our experience. Now my reluctance to leave it stems from a nagging sense that there is one more idea to express and I am not sure how it fits the character of this chronicle.

The growth of spirituality in the life of an individual is often a lonely and confusing process; seekers hunger for contact with others to confirm and clarify these often ephemeral events in their lives. I learned over many years of meditation that to share this experience is a valuable, almost indispensable, need for most of us at various times. As the writing proceeded, this conviction was strengthened.

But, spontaneously, the work has taken on deeper and broader dimensions. The writing of these spiritual episodes, no less of the transformations they effected, required a more careful examination of them. And this exploration in turn, like an archaeological dig that uncovers ever more facets of a hidden city, expands the experience, and reveals more of its evolutionary character as well as its cosmic connections. Time and again, I expressed in this writing the sublime value of the self-examined life in the fullest Platonic meaning.

In this way the evolutionary character of personal spiritual writing is revealed. As it relives the experiential milestones that marked the path, in the light of growth and accomplishment, these milestones take on a new substance and validity. A concrete recognition arises, finally, that life can be lived in happiness without sorrow, knowledge without doubt, and a future without fear.

This is not my vision. It is the revealed and promised vision of ancient Vedic seers, revealed first through oral tradition, then the hoary and obscure Vedic texts, until, at last, the arrival of the *Bhagavad Gita,* the beautiful and accessible song of the Vedas, which unabashedly describes the nature of such a life, as the following excerpts show:

> Arjuna asks: How is the man of tranquil wisdom, who abides in divine contemplation? What are his words? What is his silence? What is his work?[1]

> Krishna says: He whose mind is untroubled by sorrows, and for pleasures he has no longings, beyond passion, and fear and anger, he is the sage of unwavering mind.[2]

> Who everywhere is free from all ties, who neither rejoices nor sorrows if fortune is good or is ill, his is a serene wisdom.[3]

> There is no wisdom for a man without harmony, and without harmony there is no contemplation. Without contemplation there cannot be peace, and without peace can there be joy?[4]

> This is the Eternal in man, O Arjuna. Reaching him all delusion is gone. Even in the last hour of his life upon earth, man can reach the Nirvana of Brahman—man can find peace in the peace of his God.[5]

I use these Vedic sources deliberately. Christian, Islamic, or Judaic traditions also express these same concepts. However, their visions are so overshadowed by the experience of suffering that it has long been thought that misery is a fact of birth, to be overcome only in a post-life heavenly world. Vedic seers have, on the other hand, been an unambiguous light for millennia, denying this need for suffering, and guiding and instructing all those who are making their first hesitant, baby steps out of the bonds of spiritual ignorance.

For more than twenty years, I have been a faithful practitioner of Transcendental Meditation (TM), the spiritual practice taught by Maharishi Mahesh Yogi, from the Shankara tradition of northern India. But I have also been a student, admirer, and fraternal devotee of the myriad traditions speaking to and illuminating the lives of countless others. As I feel Maharishi's secure place in my heart, I know that the same feeling is present in the hearts of all seekers for their own paths. Therefore, I feel free to use Maharishi as a modern Master (the "world Master" to quote one of his close disciples) to elucidate the practical Vedic wisdom in modern terms for all without the fear of diminishing another tradition, knowing others can speak likewise out of their own hearts.

Speaking on January 12, 1975, inaugurating the Dawn of the Age of Enlightenment, Maharishi said:

> We started out eighteen years ago on the basis of the experience given to us by Guru Dev, telling the world, "Life is bliss" and "No man need suffer any more." It was a surprise to the world how we could dare to say this when everywhere life was suffering and struggle. But we knew that bliss was unbounded, deep within, so we advised the people to turn their attention inward, to experience that unbounded wholeness of life and bring the mind out, fully saturated with that. The people, even not believing our words, started [TM]. And once they started, the experience was there. Like that, from individual to individual the experience spread in the midst of those expressions, "life is bliss" and "No man need suffer any more." [6]

In the midst of the tumult and chaos of the modern world these words sound a stark and unreal contrast. But to me, there is nothing more real. And as they resonate and stir every atom of my being I am sure they resonate and stir the deepest recesses of the millions of spiritual seekers from all traditions, from all religions, from all cultures, New Age and old, ancient souls and those freshly minted.

So it can be asked, as it often is with insight and compassion, how can an individual be content and happy in such a world as described daily by newspaper and television? And the answer can only be: one does not end suffering by suffering; one ends suffering by joy, the joy that comes from the experiential knowledge of a real transcendent world that enlivens God's intelligence written into the genetic code of every human being, and heals thereby both spirit and body. This is the practical role of spiritual activity.

For countless generations the lonely searcher for union with this hidden realm was driven on two levels: first, his own need to fill that emptiness so deeply sensed and so poorly seen; and second, when this was finally achieved, permanently or intermittently, to see the power of that personal transformation reflected in social change. Although there is belief and faith that this reflection would indeed occur, he could not with the same conviction and surety know that the world at large also reaped these deeply felt personal benefits.

Now, in modern times, Maharishi's TM/Sidhi program has established a rock-solid foundation to sustain the faith that the order and coherence established in individuals through spiritual practice does, indeed, reflect in the larger environment. When large groups of meditators practice their "program" together the personal transcendental contact they experience radiates outward in measured and predicted ways. Social parameters shift in a more orderly direction, and personal growth finds ultimate fulfillment in this purposeful effort to create an ideal society. No longer is this dream a matter of faith; the documented evidence exists, it is available to all, and it is compelling.[7]

On this note, that nagging sense of noncompletion is put to rest. I feel I have no more to say. I greet all my fellow spiritual seekers and fold my hands in the ancient expression of Namaste, acknowledging the divine within each. And with my own family of TM meditators, I say softly, echoing Maharishi,

Jai Guru Dev[8]

NOTES

Introduction

1. Thomas Merton, *The Wisdom of the Desert*, p.9.
2. Abraham H. Maslow, *The Farthest Reaches of Human Nature*, p.295.
3. Ibid. p.295.
4. Ibid. p.314.
5. Abraham H. Maslow, *Religions, Values, and Peak-Experiences*, p.19.
6. William James, *The Varieties of Religious Experience*, p.293.
7. Abraham H. Maslow, *Religions, Values, and Peak-Experiences*, p.84.
8. William James, *The Varieties of Religious Experience*, p.293.
9. Abraham H. Maslow, *Religions, Values, and Peak-Experiences*, p.60.

Chapter I: Initiation

1. Christopher Isherwood, *My Guru and His Disciple*, p.19-20.

Chapter III: The Formative Years

1. *Great Dialogues of Plato*, p.42.

Chapter IV: The Preparatory Years

1. Maharishi Mahesh Yogi, *The Science of Being and the Art of Living*, p.130,131.

Chapter V: Foundations

1. *The Upanishads*, translated by Swami Prabhavananda and Frederick Manchester. p.51.

2. W.T. Stace, *Mysticism and Philosophy*, p.86.

3. Teresa of Avila, *Interior Castle*, p. 99.

4. C.G. Jung, *Modern Man in Search of a Soul*, p. 197.

5. Ibid. p. 204.

6. Juan Mascaro, *The Bhagavad Gita*, p.9.

7. Christopher Isherwood, *My Guru and His Disciple*, p.33.

8. Ibid. p.335.

9. Paramahansa Yogananda, *Autobiography of a Yogi*, 257.

10. Ibid. p.257.

11. Ibid. p.339.

12. Daya Mata, *Introduction to Man's Eternal Quest*, p.xiii.

13. Ibid. p.465.

14. "Deep Meditation," audio tape by Maharishi Mahesh Yogi recorded in 1960. Reissued, 1992 by Maharishi International University.

15. *Thirty Years Around the World*, Volume One 1957-1964. p.185.

16. Ibid. p.188.

17. Ibid. p.190.

18. Ibid. p.190.

19. Ibid. p.193.

20. Ibid. p.200.

21. Herbert Benson, *The Relaxation Response*, p.84.

22. "Seven States of Consciousness," *Modern Science and Vedic Science*, C.N. Alexander and R.W. Boyer. Vol.2, p.334.

Chapter VI: The Teachers I

1. Jane Roberts, *The Seth Material*, p.259.
2. Gina Cerminara, *Many Mansions*, p.30.
3. David Spangler, *Revelation: The Birth of a New Age*, p.21.
4. Ibid. p.21.

Chapter VIII: The Teachers II

1. Baird T. Spalding, *Life and Teachings of the Masters of the Far East*.
2. Ibid. Vol. I, Forward.
3. Ibid.
4. Maharishi International University founded by Maharishi Mahesh Yogi in 1971 and incorporated in California in 1972. Moved to Fairfield, Iowa, its present location, in 1974.
5. W.T. Stace, *Mysticism and Philosophy*, p.95,96.
6. Teresa of Avila, *Interior Castle*.
7. Elaine Pagels, *The Gnostic Gospels*, p.5.
8. Ibid. p.xix.
9. Ibid. p.xx.
10. Basil Pennington, *Daily We Touch Him*, p.45.
11. Perle Epstein, *Kabbalah*, p.158.
12. Ibid. p.161.
13. Basil Pennington, *Daily We Touch Him*, p.47.
14. Ibid. p.47.

Chapter IX: The Blessings II

Maharishi Mahesh Yogi, Meditations of Maharishi Mahesh Yogi, p.132.

Chapter X: Integration

1. Gary Zukav, *The Dancing Wu Li Masters*, p.81.
2. Ibid. p.82.

3. Ibid. p.48.
4. Ibid. p.38.
5. Ibid. p.98.
6. *Great Dialogues of Plato*, p.42.

Epilogue:

1. Juan Mascaro, *The Bhagavad Gita*, p.53, II,54.
2. Ibid. II,56.
3. Ibid. II,57.
4. Ibid. p.54 II,66.
5. Ibid. II,72.
6. Robert M. Oates, Jr. *Celebrating the Dawn*, p.225.
7. In the summer of 1994, in Washington D.C., a "National Demonstration Project," demonstrating the effects of the group practice of Maharishi's Transcendental Meditation and TM-Sidhi program, reduced by statistically significant amounts violent crime and social stress during the period of the project. For information on this project and several others, contact the

    Institute of Science, Technology and Public Policy

    Maharishi University of Management

    1000 North 4th St.

    Fairfield, IA 52557

8. An expression of gratitude to the succession of Masters who maintain the tradition of this teaching from age to age.

Bibliography

Benson, Herbert, M.D. *The Relaxation Response*. New York: Avon Books, 1975.

Bhagavad Gita,The, Trans. Juan Mascaro, New York: Penguin Books, 1962.

Cerminara, Gina. *Many Mansions*. New York: The New American Library, Inc., 1967.

Epstein, Perle. *Kabbalah*. New York: Doubleday, 1978.

Findhorn Garden. New York: Harper & Row Inc., 1975.

Isherwood, Christopher. *My Guru and His Disciple*. New York: Farrar-Straus-Giroux, 1980.

James, William. *The Varieties of Religious Experience*. New York: New American Library, 1958.

Jung, C.G. *Modern Man in Search of a Soul*, New York: Harcourt, Brace & World, Inc., 1933.

Levi. *The Aquarian Gospel of Jesus the Christ*. Ca: DeVorss & Co., 1991.

Maslow, Abraham H. *Religions, Values, and Peak-Experiences*. New York: The Viking Press, 1964.

___ *The Farthest Reaches of Human Nature*. New York: The Viking Press, 1971.

Merton,Thomas. *New Seeds of Contemplation*. New York: New Directions Publishing Co., 1961.

Neff, Mary K. *Personal Memoirs of H.P. Blavatsky*. Wheaton, Ill., The Theosophical Publishing House, 1971.

Oates, Robert M. *Celebrating the Dawn*. New York: G.P. Putnam's Sons, 1976.

Pagels, Elaine. *The Gnostic Gospels*. New York: Vintage Books, 1981.

Pennington, M. Basil. *Centering Prayer*. New York: Doubleday, 1980.

___ *Daily We Touch Him*. New York: Doubleday, 1979.

Plato, Great Dialogues of. Trans. W.H.D. Rouse, New York: New American Library, 1956.

Prabhavananda and Frederick Manchester. *The Upanishads*, New York: New American Library, 1948.

Roberts, Jane. *The Seth Material*. New Jersey: Prentice-Hall, Inc., 1970.

Spangler, David. *Revelation: The Birth of a New Age*. San Francisco: Third Rainbow Bridge, 1977.

Spalding, Baird T. *Life and Teachings of the Masters of the Far East*. Marina Del Rey, CA: De Pross & Co., 1924.

Stace, W.T. *Mysticism and Philosophy*. Los Angeles: Jeremy P Tarcher, Inc., 1960.

Sugrue, Thomas. *There is a River: The Story of Edgar Cayce*. New York: Dell Publishing Co., Inc., 1945.

Teresa of Avila. *Interior Castle*. Trans/ed. E. Allison Peers. New York: Doubleday, 1961.

Winner, Anna Kennedy. *The Basic Ideas of Occult Wisdom*. Wheaton, Ill: The Theosophical Publishing House, 1970.

Yogananda, Paramahansa. *Autobiography of a Yogi*. Los Angeles: Self-Realization Fellowship, 1973.

___ *Man's Eternal Quest*. Los Angeles: Self-Realization Fellowship, 1976.

Yogi, Maharishi Mahesh. *Meditations of Maharishi Mahesh Yogi.* New York: Bantam Books, Inc., 1968.

___ *Science of Being and the Art of Living.* New York: Meridian, 1963.

Zukav, Gary. *The Dancing Wu Li Masters.* New York: Bantam Books, 1979.

Additional Titles by Sunstar Publishing Ltd.

- *The Name Book* by Pierre Le Rouzic
ISBN 0-9638502-1-0 $15.95
Numerology/Philosophy. International bestseller. Over 9000 names with stunningly accurate descriptions of character and personality. How the sound of your name effects who you grow up to be.

- *Every Day A Miracle Happens* by Rodney Charles
ISBN 0-9638502-0-2 $17.95
Religious bestseller. 365 stories of miracles, both modern and historic, each associated with a day of the year. Universal calendar. Western religion.

- *Of War & Weddings* by Jerry Yellin
ISBN 0-9638502-5-3 $17.95
History/Religion. A moving and compelling autobiography of bitter wartime enemies who found peace through their children's marriage. Japanese history and religion.

- *Your Star Child* by Mary Mayhew
ISBN 0-9638502-2-9 $16.95
East/West philosophy. Combines Eastern philosophy with the birthing techniques of modern medicine, from preconception to parenting young adults.

- *Lighter Than Air* by Rodney Charles and Anna Jordan
ISBN 0-9638502-7-X $14.95
East/West philosophy. Historic accounts of saints, sages and holy people who possessed the ability of unaided human flight.

- *Bringing Home the Sushi* by Mark Meers
ISBN 1-887472-05-3 $21.95
Japanese philosophy and culture. Adventurous account of of an American businessman and his family living in '90s Japan.

- *Miracle of Names* by Clayne Conings
ISBN 1-887472-03-7 $13.95
Numerology and Eastern philosophy. Educational and enlightening—discover the hidden meanings and potential of names through numerology.

- *Voice for the Planet* by Anna Maria Gallo
ISBN 1-887472-00-2 $10.95
Religion/Ecology. This book explores the ecological practicality of native American practices.

- *Making $$$ At Home* by Darla Sims
ISBN 1-887472-02-9 $25.00
Reference. Labor-saving directory that guides you through the process of making contacts to create a business at home.

- *Gabriel & the Remarkable Pebbles* by Carol Hovin
ISBN 1-887472-06-1 $12.95
Children/Ecology. A lighthearted, easy-to-read fable that educates children in understanding ecological balances.

- *Searching for Camelot* by Edith Thomas
ISBN 1-887472-08-8 $12.95
East/West philosophy. Short easy-to-read, autobiographical adventure full of inspirational life lessons.

- *The Revelations of Ho* by Dr. James Weldon
ISBN 1-887472-09-6 $17.95
Eastern philosophy. A vivid and detailed account of the path of a modern-day seeker of enlightenment.

- *The Formula* by Dr. Vernon Sylvest
ISBN 1-887472-10-X $21.95
Eastern philosophy/Medical research. This book demystifies the gap between medicine and mysticism, offering a ground breaking perspective on health as seen through the eyes of an eminent pathologist.

- *Jewel of the Lotus* by Bodhi Avinasha
ISBN 1-887472-11-8 $15.95
Eastern philosophy. Tantric Path to higher consciousness. Learn to increase your energy level, heal and rejuvenate yourself through devotional relationships.

- *Elementary, My Dear* by Tree Stevens
ISBN 1-887472-12-6 $17.95
Cooking/Health. Step-by-step, health-conscious cookbook for the beginner. Includes hundreds of time-saving menus.

- *Directory of New Age & Alternative Publications* by Darla Sims
ISBN 1-887472-18-5 $23.95
Reference. Comprehensive listing of publications, events, organizations arranged alphabetically, by category and by location.

- *Educating Your Star Child* by Ed & Mary Mayhew
ISBN 1-887472-17-7 $16.95
East/West philosophy. How to parent children to be smarter, wiser and happier, using internationally acclaimed mind-body intelligence techniques.

- *No Justice* by Chris Raymondo
ISBN 1-887472-14-2 $23.95
Adventure. Based on a true story, this adventure novel provides behind the scenes insight into CIA and drug cartel operations. One of the best suspense novels of the '90s. Cloth.

- *The Symbolic Message of Illness* by Dr. Calin Pop
ISBN 1-887472-16-9 $21.95
East/West Medicine. Dr. Pop illuminates an astonishingly accurate diagnosis of our ailments and physical disorders based solely on the observation of daily habits.

- *On Wings of Light* by Ronna Herman
ISBN 1-887472-19-3 $19.95
New Age. Ronna Herman documents the profoundly moving and inspirational messages for her beloved Archangel Michael.

- *The Global Oracle* by Edward Tarabilda & Doug Grimes
ISBN 1-887472-22-3 $17.95
East/West Philosophy. A guide to the study of archetypes, with an excellent introduction to holistic living. Use this remarkable oracle for meditation, play or an aid in decision making.

- *Destiny* by Sylvia Clute
ISBN 1-887472-21-5 $21.95
East/West philosophy. A brilliant metaphysical mystery novel (with the ghost of George Washington) based on *A Course In Miracles*.

- *The Husband's Manual* by A. & T. Murphy
ISBN 0-9632336-4-5 $9.00
Self-help/Men's Issues. At last! Instructions for men on what to do and when to do it.
The Husband's Manual can help a man create a satisfying, successful marriage — one
he can take pride in, not just be resigned to.

- *Cosmic Perspective* by Harold W.G. Allen
ISBN 1-887472-23-1 $21.95
Science/Eastern philosophy. Allen, an eminent cosmologist, disproves the "Big Bang"
theory and opens new horizons with his dynamic principle of cosmic reincarnation, plus
his revolutionary insight into Christian origins, biblical symbolism and the Dead Sea
scrolls.

- *Twin Galaxies Pinball Book of World Records* by Walter Day
ISBN 1-887472-25-8 $12.95
Reference. The official reference book for all Video Game and Pinball Players—this
book coordinates an international schedule of tournaments that players can compete in
to gain entrance into this record book.

- *How to Have a Meaningful Relationship with Your Computer* by Sandy Berger
ISBN 1-887472-36-3 $18.95
Computer/Self-help. A simple yet amusing guide to buying and using a computer, for
beginners as well as those who need a little more encouragement.

- *The Face on Mars* by Harold W.G. Allen
ISBN 1-887472-27-4 $12.95
Science/Fiction. A metaphysical/scientific novel based on man's first expedition to
investigate the mysterious "Face" revealed by NASA probes.

- *The Spiritual Warrior* by Shakura Rei
ISBN 1-887472-28-2 $17.95
Eastern philosophy. An exposition of the spiritual techniques and practices of Eastern
Philosophy.

- *The Pillar of Celestial Fire* by Robert Cox
ISBN 1-887472-30-4 $18.95
Eastern philosophy. The ancient cycles of time, the sacred alchemical science and the
new golden age.

- *The Tenth Man* by Wei Wu Wei
ISBN 1-887472-31-2 $15.95
Eastern philosophy. Discourses on Vedanta—the final stroke of enlightenment.

- *Open Secret* by Wei Wu Wei
ISBN 1-887472-32-0 $14.95
Eastern philosophy. Discourses on Vedanta—the final stroke of enlightenment.

- *All Else is Bondage* by Wei Wu Wei
ISBN 1-887472-34-7 $16.95
Eastern philosophy. Discourses on Vedanta—the final stroke of enlightenment.

PUBLISHING AND DISTRIBUTING YOUR BOOK IS THIS SIMPLE...

1. Send us your completed manuscript.
2. We'll review it, and after acceptance we'll:
   - Register your book with The Library of Congress, Books in Print, and acquire International Standard Book Numbers, including UPC Bar Codes.
   - Design and print your book cover.
   - Format and produce 150 review copies.
   - Deliver review copies (with sales aids) to 20 of the nation's leading distributors and 50 major newspaper, magazine, television and radio book reviewers in the USA and Canada.
   - Organize author interviews and book reviews.
3. Once we have generated pre-orders for 1,000 books, New Author Enterprises will enter into an exclusive publishing contract offering up to 50% profit-sharing terms with the author.

PEOPLE ARE TALKING ABOUT US...

"I recommend New Author Enterprises to any new author. The start-up cost to publish my book exceeded $20,000—making it nearly impossible for me to do it on my own. New Author Enterprises' ingenious marketing ideas and their network of distributors allowed me to reach my goals for less than $4,000. Once my book reached the distributors and orders started coming in, New Author Enterprises handled everything—financing, printing, fulfillment, marketing—and I earned more than I could have with any other publisher."

Rodney Charles, best-selling author of
Every Day A Miracle Happens

PUBLISH IT NOW!

116 North Court St., Fairfield IA 52556
800-532-4734
http:/www.newagepage.com